PROPHETIC
CRACK

PUSHERS IN THE PULPIT, ADDICTS IN THE PEWS

REV. DR. JULIA M. MCMILLAN

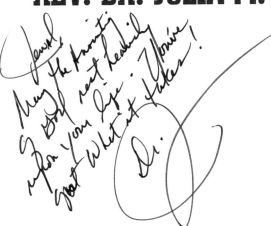

Unless otherwise noted, Scripture quotations are from the King James Version of the Bible.

Scripture quotations noted NIV are from the Holy Bible: New International Version. Copyright © 1973, 1978, 1984 International Bible Society. Used by permission. All rights reserved.

Prophetic Crack: Pushers in the Pulpit, Addicts in the Pews
ISBN: 978-0-88144-212-0
Copyright © 2010 by Dr. Julia McMillan

Published by
Thorncrown Publishing
A Division of Yorkshire Publishing Group
9731 East 54th Street
Tulsa, OK 74146
www.thorncrownpublishing.com

Printed in the United States. All rights reserved under International Copyright Law.
Cover and/or contents may not be reproduced in any manner without the express written consent of the author.

DEDICATION

This book is written with several target audiences in mind......

This book is written to the Body of Believers that comprise the church of Jesus Christ at large, who sit in churches across this world disgruntled, disconnected and discontinued...not realizing why, with hopes that revelation knowledge will inspire personal change.

This book is written to pastors and church leaders who, knowingly or unknowingly, have spent their lives exploiting innocence on the frontline by serving a demented disease of their own...an unwavering need for power and control.

This book is written to the many who, while earnestly seeking a healthy and loving relationship with the Savior, have settled for the unhealthy domination of a modern day Pharoah.

This book is dedicated to the many who have sought and found deliverance for their wounded souls, with hopes that we never forget those who yet remain under the influence.

This book is dedicated to the church I am privileged to pastor, with hopes that never in the history of our existence do we become guilty of dealing Prophetic Crack.

This book is dedicated to my family, for having stood by and supported my preparation for the exposure of "Prophetic Crack." Now you know why!!!!

God Bless!

Rev. Dr. Julia M. McMillan

CONTENTS

FOREWORD

Every institution has its own brand. Whether we sell hamburgers, fly airplanes, repair computers or operate on hearts and kidneys, every club, agency, business or group has its own unique "emotional reputation". "They do good work," we say. "They can be trusted," we muse. "They are over-priced for the quality they offer." "They are a safe bet." And on it goes.

Every institution has its own brand. And *the church is no exception.* One's "brand" has to do with the emotional and psychological "taste" that is left with a client or customer, once the service or product has been experienced. Often the discussion or response to our brand is *not verbal.* It is *visceral.* The head, the heritage, the hope may urge one toward finding a home in the church. But the 'brand' of church as a credible healing place has been damaged by certain individuals who have been left at the institutional helm: unguarded, unhealed, unchecked, and unexamined, by the gatekeepers of the church. And in our brand of Christian acquiescence these unhealed leaders reproduce themselves in every region, every denomination, in every color, gender and creed.

In our recent past, some of the church's organizational mystique has been dispelled and truth-telling has been painfully broached. Some *sexual abuse* has been aired out, and scores of boys and men (and some women) have begun the painful march toward reconciliation with themselves and the institutional church to which they were once "addicted"— by seduction or by force. *Sexism* as a soul-damaging arrangement is, bit by bit, finding its own conversation by the uninterrupted procession of women (and some men) in the church. We have refused, alas, to keep silent. *Financial betrayals* have been uncovered by the masses, as the faithful addicted themselves to electronic, evangelistic hopes of miracles and quick turns-around. "Only send that seed-offering today and there will be a miracle in 30 days" was the promise. Yet, far too often the undelivered promise fell in the blind spot of the "hooked", who kept on pouring water into buckets with holes: Unrecognized addiction.

Some of us painfully discover that there are addictions and addictive patterns that are not as easily recognized—or may never manifest— as *gender* focused, or *overtly* sexual or financial. We just know there is something chronically, excruciatingly *wrong in the way we experience our connections within the church.* These are the addictions that embed themselves in *relationships* of trust.

Relationship addictions not only embed themselves in relationships of trust...they *disrupt* relationships, they *manipulate* relationships, they ultimately *deform* relationships which were meant to nourish us. They are particularly damaging when these relationship addictions intercourse with religion. They can seem *demonic when they masquerade as representations of God.*

In her book, *Prophetic Crack,* Dr. Julia McMillan brings to the surface critical issues which have converged in this generation, and the insidious ways the issues have been left to grow, unaddressed. What happens to a generation who floods our pews looking for healing from their wounds? The wounds are barely hidden: Rejection. Father hunger. Poor parental models. Non-existent covenantal examples. Unexcavated hurts. Degraded standards. The failure of absolutes. The soul-hungers which spawn addictions.

Furthermore, what happens when that same generation has not been conditioned *to do the hard work* of reflection, confession, responsibility-taking, confrontation or authentic reconciliation? They have learned to self-medicate, or to anesthetize themselves, and to do it quickly, cheaply and without regard for the future or quality of life (The "crack-cocaine" generation). What happens when church itself becomes a drug? And what transpires when these walking wounded, these "quick-fixers" land in the hands of broken, narcissistic church *leaders* who dazzle, shine, and promise to fix them or their worlds, both now and hereafter? (Pushers). Gerald May(1988) teaches us in *Addiction and Grace* that all addictions must have an idol. A certain kind of sick leader is only too happy to fill that position. The inner 'wounded world' between pastor and member solidifies in secrecy. It is a world these leaders have never even glanced at for themselves, barely understand, and only exacerbate for others.

To put it another way, wed the social, emotional and ultimately *spiritual* cravings (users), to persons bound by the lust for power and control that is resident in the souls of gifted but broken leaders (pushers), and we have what Schaef and Fassel (1990) called *an Addictive Organization*. This destructive dance is unleashed exponentially when the pulpit is unguarded, when the walls of prayer and discernment are broken down, and when a certain use of scripture creates a *culture of silence*. For the few members who just may sniff a hint of dysfunction, or who may dare to broach the subject of toxicity in the pastor-member relationships, they are quickly rapped on the knuckles. "Touch not mine anointed, and do my prophets no harm." (I Chronicles 16:22)

For a startling number of folks in this present generation, church has become a downright dangerous place to be. Dr. McMillan's book is long overdue in the here-to-stay climate of shiny publicity, slick mega-church aspirations, hero-worship and charismatic but unbroken, unexamined, independent preachers. It is overdue especially (but not exclusively) for a generation of folks who often come to the church out of contexts of gross dysfunction, and too often, from addictive families. We chose our religious leaders naively and are forgiving long after judgment and justice should have been pronounced.

May this book call us back to health. May it dare us to examine the patterns which we bring from the world into the church, and the pain we remain comfortable with long after our sins have been forgiven. Patterns of mindless addiction help us feel momentarily distracted from our present pain. Patterns of control, manipulation and seduction help us feel falsely secure. Both will continue as long as we (leaders) can get away with it, and as long as members turn away from the prophetic voices that cut across our own denial. Dr. Julia McMillan is one such voice.

Finally, we must herald the hundreds of pastors, preachers and church leaders who quietly serve God's people and whose only hope is to be, not famous, but *faithful*. They are the ones who push others on to growth and self-actualization, on to destiny, on to becoming new in Christ. They are the ones who suffer from the bad press and the sick behavior of the few. These are the pastors and church leaders who study, pray, serve, use no gimmicks, and quietly wonder why their churches do not grow beyond a few dozen. They are the ones who are honest, hard-working, reflective and ...yes, *holy* men and women of God. In the still moments they have watched the "prosperity" of the questionable, and observed the crowds stream into the churches of the less scrupulous. If this book comes into your hands, may it warn you away from the soul-shrinking emotions of anger, control, and manipulation which could tempt even the best of us, after long years of too-slow success and Teflon members. May Dr. McMillan's insights give you comfort and enlightenment in knowing that some broken, addicted, church-wounded soul may end up at your door. And *you* may be their last hope to get them to the Blood.

Redeem the brand.

Claudette Anderson Copeland, D.Min
New Creation Christian Fellowship
San Antonio, Texas
January 2009

ACKNOWLEDGEMENTS

No victory in life is without the sum total of efforts and sacrifices of many, some known, some unknown. This book is no different. It is with great gratitude that I acknowledge the labors and experiences of those without whose contributions, *Prophetic Crack* would not be possible.

First, thank you to a strong sister whose testimony gives us the privilege of depicting the true and lived experience of a "crack addict." You are awesome and your continued recovery is our prayer.

Secondly, to those victims whose confessions expose the realities of the painful aftermath of church abuse. Thank you for your testimonies and thank you for your transparency.

Thirdly, to the many who sat up late with me as I pondered and prayed, laboring to complete my assignment. You know who you are! For your lives I am eternally grateful.

Fourthly, to my husband, Terry McMillan and my children whose patience and understanding, as I travailed through the process of preparation, has been the incredible force that has motivated and carried me. For you, I am eternally grateful.

To my mentor, Dr. Claudette Anderson Copeland, thanks for your belief in my voice and your endearing commitment to the cause of Christ.

To our Lord, for entrusting me with the safety of delivering the legible discourse intended specifically to "Set the Captives Free!"

PROPHETIC CRACK

"But Elymas the sorcerer (for so is his name by interpretation) withstood them, seeking to turn away the deputy from the faith. Then Saul, (who also is called Paul,) filled with the Holy Ghost, set his eyes on him. And said, O full of all subtilty and all mischief, thou child of the devil, thou enemy of all righteousness, wilt thou not cease to pervert the right ways of the Lord?" (Acts 13: 8-10)

Sorcery! The very sound of the word rushes to thoughts of darkened rooms, occult rituals, voodoo, black magic, evil spirits, and poor, unsuspecting victims entranced by supernatural powers. While this imagery is all very true, there is another kind of sorcery that few people are aware of, one that has deceived many, many people, including myself.

This type of sorcery is an unhealthy spiritual entanglement and is far more deceptive than voodoo and black magic or the mystical darkness of the underworld. It deeply damages the spirit of anyone it touches. It is so detestable in the eyes of God that He warns that sorcerers will spend eternity in the fiery sea of burning sulfur. I was cruising down this broad road of destruction, ignorant of the practices I was so dangerously influenced by. They were practices of manipulation, domination and control, and they came from the people I trusted the most.

Since the early days of the first church, there has been an active presence of deception and trickery. Elymas, the sorcerer, symbolizes satanic opposition that is present everywhere and at all times, often seated in high places. The proconsul, or governor, was literally under Elymas's influence. Sad to say that even today, there are officers and rulers with tremendous power and authority, terribly influenced by powers of darkness and wickedness, and as my experience has taught me, many don't even know it.

Acts 13:8-10 is the very first time in scripture that Saul is called Paul. By all accounts, Paul was a very mild mannered man in many ways, but when he encountered *this* kind of opposition, against the word of God, he not only recognized it, but exposed it with all that was in him. He charged it to Satan and he denounced it, and we today must do the same! *"Have nothing to do with the fruitless deeds of darkness, but rather expose them!"* (Ephesians 5:11)

The travesty in today's society is that many who discern wickedness, trickery and darkness (especially in the church) are afraid to confront it! For fear of being ostracized or rejected, many recognize the opposition but rarely, if ever, expose it. Thus, we have learned to accept it. We have learned how to live with it and have mastered how to cover it up. Our skills have become intrinsically embedded so much so, that we accept as right that which we know to be wrong, we accept as pure that which we know to be filthy, and we accept as truth that which we know to be a lie. Deception from the father of lies has won—even in the church!!! It has all but paralyzed truth and has silenced any confession of sin. Wow, and isn't that exactly what addictions do? And to think that even professing Christians can become victims of internal addictions, affected heavily by the idols of their affections, so much so that our very doctrine can so easily be compromised. And that's the same center of thought that surrounds the mind of the drug addict: Deceived by the grandeur, accepted as pure and proper behavior, and compromised by the immoral and unscrupulous character of the moment. Addiction is a wicked force that causes even the best of us to waive our rights to live holy. Its indelible influence dominates the very core of truth and manipulates the life out of reason. This book seeks to expose the root of this demonic parasite, which clings to its predators as does a dominating and deadly bacteria.

Elymas's main concern was the preservation of his source of wealth, (the lavish generosity of Sergus Paulus), his power over the proconsul (who was himself a very important man, a high administrator over an assigned territory), and his pride regarding his own "presumed wisdom." In short, Elymas was motivated by *"the lust of the flesh, the lust of the eyes, and the pride of life"* (1 John 2:16). It was not in effect what Elymas *had*, but what *had* him! Self-preservation, coupled with perceived power and pride—what a dangerous combination!

And thus the travesty in the modern church....self-preservation coupled with a perceived power and pride, masqueraded under the guise of ecclesiastical authority. The church is, in many ways, a hot mess! The irony, though, is that many church leaders did not start out this way. Many had great and honorable intentions at the start of their ministries. So what happened? What caused the shift from authentic ministry to ambitious profitability? How did this demonic spirit invade the church?

The following pages seek to explore the seed of wickedness and deceit that has become the pervasive description of the modern church that has contaminated innocent lives, become the default for otherwise unsuccessful business men and women and all but paralyzed the power, presence and person of Almighty God.

The Greek word for "church" is *ekklesia*, which means an assembly. In Acts 19:39, 41, it is used for any large group of people. But among Christians, the word *ekklesia* came to have a special meaning: all who believe in Jesus Christ. When Luke writes in Acts 5:11 that "great fear seized the whole church," he is not talking about an assembly, but all believers in Christ. The church in its original use referred to a people, not a building. "Christ loved the church and gave himself up for her" (Ephesians 5:25). Christ gave himself for a people, not a building. So, the true definition of church, elevates the person over the property.

Today, we know the church to exist at many levels. At one level is the universal church, which includes everyone worldwide who accepts Jesus Christ as Lord and Savior. Whether in China, India, or the USA, globally, we are in partnership together for the cause of Christ. At another level is the local church, from storefront to mega, consisting of a body of believers who regularly meet together. This meeting together is to promote fellowship. (*1 John 1:7*) Fellowship comes from the Greek word, *koinonia,* which means "to share in common." Christian fellowship must be more than attending church; it must also promote unity of the body in love and faith. The local church is designed to do just that.

Legally, our government defines the church as a recognized body, with a creed and a documented form of worship, with a distinct ecclesiastical governing body, a membership, and regular religious services. Because the church is a legal entity it must operate according to sound business practices. Financial services have benefited greatly from putting churches in legal and financial order. As such, certain fiscal and legal criteria define the church. These are required and expected, but not at the expense of the primary design of the local church.

This writing is primarily about the local church. We know that a local congregation is designed to give us a sense of belonging, and of being involved with other believers. It can give us some spiritual safety, so that we are not blown around by strange ideas, philosophies, or doctrines. The congregation can give us friendship, fellowship and encouragement. It is the process through which we as Christians receive our sanctification. The local church is designed to minister to the needs of the broken, to attract the lost, and to encourage believers. It is to be a beloved community, with sacrificial giving so that nothing or no one is lacking. In addition, God has given us different gifts and abilities, and he wants us to work together "for the common good" (1 Corinthians 12:4-7); and for the building of the body for the work of the ministry (Ephesians 4:11). Primarily, that work consists of winning other souls for Christ through the message of the gospel. This is the ideal for every leader to ascribe to, and every member to seek after.

It doesn't matter if the church is small or mega. The atmosphere should be the trusted beloved community of believers. Small or mega, the leaders must be able to facilitate an atmosphere of love, fellowship, right living, and equipping of the saints, freedom in Christ, growth and maturity. Yet, not all churches are successful: some meet a few goals well, while failing miserably at others. Prophetic Crack attempts to give enough information for leaders and congregants to know when their church is under the enemy's attack, particular in the areas of legalism, materialism, emotionalism, and manipulation of God's word. It behooves us all to recognize the subtle traps of the enemy.

Satan has always come against the church. The history of the persecution of Christians has been sufficiently documented. From the Roman persecution with martyrs, lions, spears, and chains to modern day persecution with executions, church burnings, and political restrictions, we know and understand that Satan is still persecuting the church. Western Christians come under more subtle persecution. For example, persons adopting a philosophy called Secular Humanism hold science and facts over faith and the supernatural. They move on school policies so that prayers can be taken from school; religious holidays can be taken off the calendar; and students are not to hear the creation story—not even as an alternative to Darwinism. Even more subtle is the fact that even among great churches, there are pushers in the pulpit and addicts in the pews!

By paralleling the life of the crack-addicted, this book will explore the aspects that contribute to organizational addiction and the process of emotional, spiritual and physical detachment. Pushers in the pulpit and addiction in the pews are as common as a church on every street corner. By careful investigation of the seed of this wickedness, *Prophetic Crack* seeks to expose the underlying reasons that so many parishioners are oblivious to.

The book is divided into three trains of thought. After the Introduction, in Confessions of a Crack Addict, I present a true story of Ms. M, a recovering addict who volunteered to be interviewed for this work. Chapters two through four explore the causes and results of addiction. Chapters five through seven explore the seed of its control and the devastation of its impact. Chapters eight through twelve explore the awakening and response to the burden of addiction.

The sting is venomous. The wounds are visceral. The mark is permanent. But God!

CHAPTER ONE

CONFESSIONS OF
A CRACK ADDICT
(UNDERSTANDING THE ADDICTION)

The people that I hung around with, I saw them doing it. I liked what I saw. After I hung around the people for a while, I just started. I figured, if I can't beat them, I might as well join them. They looked like they were having fun. They looked like they had life in control.

This would only last for a little while. After a time, I watched the drugs begin to bring them down. I watched very confident and strong people being brought to shame and disgrace. I was under the impression that I could handle it. It won't get me. I can do this. I can handle this. I'm stronger than they are. It won't do me like that. But after a while, after about two years, yes, it did. For a while, I handled it, but soon after, it started handling me.

It was the money. I saw people who were using and selling, and they always had money, so, I thought I would take the chance and do the same. These were my friends. They wouldn't lead me astray. I was always the type who needed to be connected. Friends and relationships were important so, whatever the risk, I was willing to do it...for the sake of my friends. But then after a while, the whole drug scene started wrecking my life... not just me, but my whole family.

By now it had me. I knew I was addicted when I started taking from my family, my grandchildren, my mother, my children, and anybody else who had something that would supply my needs. In my case, basically I took from my family. They were easy to take from after all I would say, "they won't hurt me." It was safe to take from them. Yes, it's okay for me to do this. Then I became very selfish. When I would get mine, I would shy away from everybody. I didn't want to share my hit. I just wanted to be by myself and just do my own thing. Then it all backfired.

Because I hurt my family so bad, they started shying away from me. My mother wouldn't let me come into her house. One of my girls just didn't want no part of me, period. And I felt like okay, they don't want to be bothered with me. What else do I have? I didn't have anywhere to go so, I just stayed in the streets and just continued and continued and continued. In my eyes my family had rejected me. They had turned their backs on me and wanted nothing else to do with me. So, at that time, my new family became those who were doing the same thing I was.....using and selling drugs. I knew it was wrong but it was now my life and the only thing I had to live for. The streets became my life and the addicts became my family. They understood me. They could identify with my pain. We all had something in common...we were hurt, we were broken, we were hopeless and we were homeless.

I had to support myself. At that time I used to always say, I forgot I even had feet because I stayed on my back so much in order to support my habit. This man, that man, you know, whatever. Yeah, it didn't matter who, where or nothing. I would do anything….whatever it took…anything.

My brother was a heroin addict. He would always tell me, don't do this, don't do that. But I would say, "you're doing it, why can't I?" He was addicted for years until finally, he was killed during a drug-related crime. Yeah, he was my oldest brother. There were only three of us. I was real hurt when my brother died, but even after his death, I continued to use. I would rationalize my addiction.

I used to say, "Well, it must be okay because if God didn't want me to have it, He wouldn't have put it here for me." I now know that was just dumb! But at the time, drugs were satisfying my needs. I was very lonely, I'd been rejected by those I thought loved and understood me, I was hurt…what else was I supposed to do. God must have sent this to me. Every time I needed more, it was there for me so I just thought this was God's way of taking care of me. I was very confused.

The drugs meant everything to me. One time, I was so busy searching to get a hit that I mistakenly got in a car with a man I thought I knew. I didn't know him at all… he told me off, and he had his way with me, then he told me to get out of his car. He put a butcher knife against my neck and told me to walk back to where I came from. And that still didn't stop it. Abuse…physically, emotionally, and sexually….but that still didn't stop it. It had taken over my life. The drugs even came before my children. I loved my children, but the drugs came first. My girls were teenagers then and needed me so much. But the drugs had to come first. I knew then, that they had me for real.

I couldn't keep a job, I couldn't do anything. I wouldn't even try to look for one so I began to steal to support my habit. One night I went into a three-story apartment complex, and laid flat on the nasty floor to have sex with a guy for crack, and then it got to the point that that's where I was sleeping, on the stairwell, and that's where I would sleep and wake up next to someone I didn't know from Adam, half the time.

Not all of them were pushers. Some of them were men who smoked crack themselves, the majority of them. This one guy, he would go and rob people or take from the pusher and he would come back and it was there and that was it.

Life at that time meant nothing. I didn't even think about it. Whatever happened was okay. It was okay. I'm still living so it must be okay! I used to wish I was dead. I often wondered why I kept going through this. I knew it was wrong. But at the time, I couldn't get out. I didn't know how to get out. Several times I tried to hurt myself to try to get out. But even that didn't work. When I would get down, somebody would always pop up with something. Another hit...Another hit. It became normal. I was surviving from day to day and my needs were being met. Why change it?

People around me wanted me to change, namely my mother. She sent me through a lot of treatment. They would say fake it until you make it and that's what I did. When I was done with my program I would say, I'm fine; I can go back and do this again. But each time it got worse and worse.

I thought that the life I was living was real. There was this guy. We were together a lot. Sometimes he would go home and he would leave me out there by myself. I thought it was fine. I thought it was a real relationship. I thought it was a stable relationship because he made sure when he did come around I had what I wanted. I thought that was what a relationship was supposed to be. Take care of what I want. I shouldn't expect anymore than that. I was so confused.

I would tell the people I was with that I'd had enough, but they didn't care. Every time I would say I wanted out, they just gave me more crack. "Smoke this with me, you'll be all right." They would make me feel special so I wouldn't think about trying to break free. They made me depend on them. In fact, they would ask me to help them, so it made me feel needed. I knew everybody so I could help them get rid of their product. I became an asset to them. I found out they were my worst nightmare!

Sometimes I would be sleep, like I said I went to sleep anywhere, it didn't matter, and they would come and wake me up. They would want me to just sit there with them and draw customers to them. For my pay, I could smoke as much as I wanted. I have smoked crack on the stairs of the church. I was sick.

At that time I didn't care about going to jail. In fact, I was ready to go to jail. Jail was a safe place for me. I could regroup, get fed, and have a decent shower. I was ready for whatever it would take to get me off the streets.

Then I met the last straw. I took a woman's purse; it was around Christmas time. She had money to buy her children toys. And I took it. And somebody told her I took it because they had seen me with the purse. They came looking for me...to kill me. I went into a three-story building and fell on my knees. I screamed and hollered, Lord save me. Rescue me please!! I don't want to do this no more!! Help me, somebody's going to kill me! They found me. They held a gun on me and told me to walk out of the building. When I walked out of the building they held a pistol to my head until the police came. Instead of taking my life, they saved it. The police rescued me from the hands of my enemies. Getting caught was the best thing to ever happen to me.

I stayed in jail about a month. After that, I was done. I had hit rock bottom. I had been in jail time and time again. My mother had sent me to treatment centers, she would have me locked up for months and months and I would get out and do the same thing because I had not thought about my life and what could happen to me. This time would be different.

Think about it. The people who were about to kill me told me to go sit down and that they were calling the police. Suddenly their minds changed and they went from wanting to kill me to wanting to send me to jail...which is exactly where I wanted to go. When I was in that building somehow my mind disconnected. Now I was feeling it was time to physically disconnect. I could feel myself turning away from that which had had me for so long. Finally, I was ready to break free and to get clean. I had detoxed before, but this time was different. I wanted a new life, for real.

I stayed in jail until I detoxed. Finally I went before the judge to face what I had done. He wanted to give me three years' probation. I thought, "I can't do that." One of the girls that had been on the streets with me said yes, you can. At that point the judge said to me, if I violated these three years, he would send me to prison for 10 years. He said, either probation or isolation.

That's all it took. From that day on, I got into the church. I was still beat up and confused. One of my daughters took me in. I was faithful to my program and I was committed to staying clean. That was 12 years ago. 12 years ago!

I knew it would be hard to stay clean and I knew I couldn't do it alone. I had to refocus my life. At that time my motivation came from my mother. Her health was deteriorating and I didn't want her to pass away with me in prison or on the streets. I wanted her to see me clean. I needed for her to believe in me again. I needed for my children and grandchildren to believe in me again. The thought of them all having to live with me addicted again was too painful to bear. They were my motivation. They were my real family and I knew now that I had to live for them.

My mother lived for the next five years and I was clean! My children and I were able to reestablish our bond. They learned how to trust me again. This was all I wanted to begin with. I wanted a life of real love and trust. Love and trust gave me a better life, the life I was created for.

My strength now comes from God and God alone. I stay in my Bible. I'm in church. And that's it, by the grace of God. It is by His grace that I am able to tell my story. I could have been dead. I should have been dead. Now I am able to keep a job and buy nice things when I have extra money. I am able to dress up and go to church...all because of the grace of God. When I had money I used to take it to my pusher, looking at him dressing nice while I was looking like a tramp. But now that is what keeps me on my job, my Bible, my church and my family, my family, my family, yeah.

At first I thought it would be tough living clean but I found out that the devil can't do anything with a made up mind! My mind was made up. Even when I would think about going back, I'd quickly be reminded that what's behind me almost killed me. I have nothing to live for but my future...what lies ahead. That wasn't working. This is. This is where I will be!

By the grace of God I am here and I believe that God will give back to me all that the locusts have stolen....my mind, my faith, my children, my integrity, my pride, my esteem, my life. I love God too much and He's brought me too far to turn around now!

It has been 12 years that Ms. M has been clean and I praise God and thank Him for that. She was able to break that vicious cycle. It did not transfer to her children. It did not transfer to her grandchildren. And now she is living a clean life, resurrected again and so now we, the church, are able to walk with her in the new dawn of her life.

CHAPTER TWO

MAGICAL SEDUCTION
(UNDERSTANDING THE BAIT)

*"See to it that no one takes you captive through philosophy and
empty deception, according to the tradition of men, according
to the elementary principles of the world rather than according
to Christ"* (Colossians 2:8)

Paul is warning the church in Colossi that believers should
not be taken captive, in mind, body, soul, or substance through
the empty deceit of philosophy blended with Christianity. The
apostle condemns this because, in his words, the mixture of the
word plus human wisdom was empty and deceitful, promising
happiness, but giving none.

To deliberately mislead or misguide the minds of the
vulnerable has to be among the most detestable of sins. To take
advantage of one's mind by making of it a playground for the
known misrepresentation of truth is to participate in the art of
deception. Paul's burden is that believers not fall prey to this
destructive act and he therefore posts an all-out warning!
Beware! Paul knew of the proclivity of false representations of
Christ by way of church leaders, and so he is deliberate as he
warns the believer.

He is warning the believer to be careful of this act of trickery. He begs them not to be taken captive; not to be taken "hostage" in their minds, in their bodies, in their souls and in their substance by those who specialize in the practice of deception. Paul is aware of charismatic tactics—the oracle blend of empty philosophy, linguistic domination and Christianity. Paul says these practices are grounded not on solid reasoning but rather on the traditions of men. Their primary purpose is to trap and ensnare.

Being taken captive, ensnared, imprisoned, and enslaved is the daily experience of a person who is in the grips of drug addiction. And no drug entraps and ensnares better in our modern era than crack cocaine. Crack cocaine is a form of powdered cocaine that swept the underclass communities of the country in the mid '80s causing devastation, particularly to African-American families. Crack is derived from the residue of cooked powdered cocaine mixed with water and other substances, the most common of which are ammonia or baking soda. The hardened substance is crushed into small pieces called rocks and smoked by its users. The first thing you must understand about crack cocaine is that it causes immediate euphoric (exhilarating) experiences when used (albeit, temporary) and serves as an escape from the conditions of life. It is a wonder drug! It chemically covers physical and emotional pain and alters the mind's perception of reality. It makes its users feel high, numb, and content. Like caffeine, cocaine produces wakefulness and reduces hunger. The user usually loses weight effortlessly, and would in fact, prefer to smoke than to eat, drink, or have sex. Psychological effects include feelings of well-being and a grandiose sense of power and ability mixed with anxiety and restlessness. As the drug wears off, these temporary sensations of mastery are at times replaced by an intense depression, even suicidal thoughts and severe paranoia. Thus, the user craves another hit. (Narconon International)

No one wants to be a drug addict; they're not born with this ambition, but this doesn't stop people from getting addicted. The most commonly asked question is simply - how? How could my son, daughter, father, mother, sister, or brother become so dependent on something they know to be harmful to them? How could this happen? And why won't they stop?

You read earlier the confessions of Ms. M, a recovering addict. She is but one of millions who have been taken captive by this thing called base, chalk, rock— crack. What lured her into a life where the rock that she knew best was not the rock of ages but crack cocaine?

What was her bait? If you know anything about fishing, you know the bait is the most important component of a successful fishing trip. In fact, you can have all the right equipment, but without the right bait, an unsuspecting fish will never bite the hook. Some bait looks alive, shiny, and just safe enough to capture for a hungry fish at feeding time. What was Ms. M's bait?

For Ms. M, the bait was the inner emotions of wanting to be accepted by peers. And the lure of quick and easy money to improve her economically challenged lifestyle. Her friends seemed to be able to handle smoking and selling crack, so much so, she became convinced that she could do it, too. She had a need that the drug fulfilled; it had an appeal, and looked safe enough to meet her needs.

While some drugs gradually lead to an unhealthy dependency that has both physiological and psychological components, there is nothing gradual about crack cocaine addiction. Crack cocaine is known for its quick addictive properties. What starts as today's fun, ends as a nightmare just a few hits later. One day, Ms. M was smoking to be social and selling to make ends meet, and just two weeks later she became a functioning addict, craving and compromising for "a hit." Addiction to crack cocaine is powerful and uneasy to break. Like a bad marriage to a partner who loves you passionately and abuses you miserably, cocaine creates a compulsive need and enslaves the desires of the user; holding all logic, morality, responsibility, and healthy living captive.

In addition to acting quickly on the physiological system, crack cocaine activates the brain's reward systems, releasing dopamine—a pleasure chemical in the brain. The promise of reward is very intense, causing the individual to crave the drug and to focus their activities around taking the drug. Drugs also reduce a person's level of consciousness, interfering with the ability to think or be fully aware of present circumstances. After extended use, the person no longer responds to the drug in the way that person initially responded. That is, the person develops a tolerance in which increasingly more of the same drug is needed to attain the original desired effect. Before you know it, they have swallowed the bait, and are caught up in a nightmare called addiction!

Church members also have been known to swallow the bait. As it relates to the church, people are attracted to something that draws them into a euphoric experience, often laced with emotionalism, only to discover that the effect is short-lived. But just as with cocaine, the promise of reward is intense, and therefore causes the individual to crave the experience so much that they crave and focus all their activities around seeking the next "spiritual high," i.e., "taking the drug!"

In addition, for crack cocaine to be attractive to a person, there commonly must first be some underlying unhappiness, sense of hopelessness, or physical pain. Interestingly, people seek churches for relief from the same underlying unhappiness, hopelessness and varying degrees and types of pain. In search of healing, they long for the antidote that will kill their realities or alter their situations. Often, as with crack, the worship experience is seen as extremely pleasurable, though short-lived. After the benediction, "the drug" soon wears off, and the parishioners return to their same hopeless state, awaiting the midweek fix (Bible study) or the next Sunday's service (hit!). Hooked on the feelings of temporary hope and well-being, parishioners return again and again. The pews are full of vulnerable people— susceptible to the damaging effects of addiction.

Addiction threatens to control, manipulate and dominate; it matters not if that addiction is to crack cocaine or to the excitement of church life.

Crack cocaine is a very harmful and abusive drug disguised as excitement and pleasure. It's a cheap thrill and it preys on the vulnerable, and the weak, as it lures its users into counterfeit experiences. Its extended danger lies in its power to create an insatiable desire to be used more and more. Captive users become familiar with the drug, and deceive themselves that they have mastered its effects, even though enslaved by that which is harmful and debilitating — they crave more!

So far, I have suggested two common types of bait—the quick action of the drug's addictive properties and the immediate and extreme pleasure of the drug. When these two lures merge with the vulnerability of the addict, then the effects are addictive. How can the allure of such a deadly drug addiction be at all comparable to the allure that draws the addict to the pew? I know from firsthand experience that there are in fact, uncanny comparisons. My name is Julia M. McMillan, and I am a former church-addict.

I was looking for a church home. I'd been in church all of my life, and to be without a church home was almost like a fish on dry land trying to live and survive. So my husband and I had been visiting churches all over the city—we were new to the city, had been here approximately three or four months, and had yet to find the place where we needed to be. I was about 28 or 29 at the time. We had a two-year-old son, and my husband's job had transferred him here about a month before we arrived. So, I desperately needed a church home. I wanted to connect with some people who could identify with where we were— climbing the corporate ladder, if you will. And so, we had visited churches all over the city, and then finally we walked into the doors of one, and felt like this was it. We did not know exactly what we were looking for. But of all the other places we visited, whether we knew what we were looking for or not, we knew what was *not* "it." And so we made no commitments to any of them.

But then we met a church, a congregation that seemed to meet our needs, and at the time did. They were family-oriented; lots of young families and the like. Music was hyped—and music was a major part of our life at that time. The Word appeared solid and it just appeared to be a place where we could grow and develop and mature into what God had called us to be. When we went there, the people (the way they were dressed, what they drove—yes, that was important—they way they looked) all those kinds of things seemed to match us. We were corporate people at the time. Leadership was corporate-minded, and it just seemed to be a major, exceptionally great fit for us. Therefore, shortly after the first visit we joined. They had a wonderful, thriving children's ministry, so they had activities for our son—so, it was the place for the McMillan family to be. We were enticed by the ministries. Not just the Children's ministry, but the Men's ministry, the Women's ministry, and the Couple's ministry, to name a few. These ministries seemed to address the needs of families, but not just any family, our family!

Now, I was broken—I was extremely broken. Right before I came to that church, I lost my dearest friend in North Carolina to cancer. She, at the time, was in her 60s. She was one of my first and most cherished mentors. I was not grieving properly concerning her and had extreme emotional issues at the time. I needed some place that would offer what I needed to hear and would help me to survive that difficult time. I needed a quick and exciting fix. Though I never shared the state of my condition when I came to the church with anyone, I knew what it was, and I knew what I was wrestling with—all which was very secretive to others around me. I was brilliant, I was young, and I was a gifted woman, with energy, and charisma, and therefore brought some things to the church that could be used right away to keep me too busy to ever have to deal with my own issues.

That was my state when I came—a state of vulnerability. The church was alluring—a formidable, irresistible bait. I was enticed by the corporate aura; I was enticed by the mid-level management congregation of people who appeared to be on the same journey as my husband and I were in our corporate climb at the time; but equally so, I was enticed by the music. Because I sing and love praise and worship, the music was very alluring. Both pastors at the time sang and led praise and worship. In fact they were key figures in major choirs –I had even heard some of their music before arriving. My Lord, what a wonderful fit! I was captivated!!

My experience is not uncommon. It, in fact, typifies the lure of mega-churches all around the country. To hold the attention of young adults, with corporate backgrounds and the gifts you "need" for ministry, some leaders try to strike a balance between what God requires for His church and what man requires for his corporation. If one errs and caters to the demand of the latter, the church is endangered by the traditions of men.

> *"He answered and said unto them, 'Well has Esaias prophesied of you hypocrites, as it is written, This people honors me with their lips, but their heart is far from me. Howbeit in vain do they worship me, teaching for doctrines the commandments of men. For laying aside the commandment of God, you hold the tradition of men, as the washing of pots and cups: and many other such like things you do.' And he said unto them, 'Full well you reject the commandment of God, that you may keep your own tradition.'"* Mark 7:6-9 (See also Matt 15:7-9)

Christian Liberties.Com, published an article on authoritarianism in the church, called *"Should Pastors Rule Over You."* Note their words regarding the "traditions of men"!

"It's no secret that many "Christian" churches have become abusive businesses disguised as churches, run by CEOs disguised as shepherds. Churches like this prey on the vulnerable and unwary, and cater to human selfishness in order to attract and recruit members. Those in the world can usually see this far easier than most Christians who are usually too close to the problem to recognize it. Sad to say, many people have turned away from faith in Jesus Christ and want nothing more to do with Christianity in general because of the pain and suffering that they have endured at the hands of these so-called "churches" and their counterfeit leaders. Jesus gets blamed for the folly of rebellious men (and women) who refuse to adhere to the clear teachings of the Bible. Instead, these false leaders teach their own ideas, theories and opinions as if they were the truth and the clear commands of Christ." (Howey)

While I did not think the church or its leaders were counterfeit, they were powerful, alluring, and teetering towards creating new traditions that appealed to young adults. This serves as a caution for pastors and leaders who may be tempted to teach modern culture rather than the Bible. There are addicts in the pews who have come to the house of God with real needs, including the primary need to know the Lord in spirit and in truth, without wooing with flash and flair.

So far, I have mentioned the corporate congregation, the ministries, and the music. What are some other enticements of the church in general and the "mega church" in particular? Well, there are several seductive and pervasive dynamics that affect many and are directly related to the making of church addicts. Some of these have been thoroughly discussed by other writers referenced throughout this book. What you see here is a short list of what I believe to be the top six lures after extensive reading and investigation and based on my own experience.

1. Capitalism
2. Corporate Structure
3. Recognition of Gifts
4. Professional Networks
5. Entertainment/Programs/Productions
6. Perceived Power

Lure # 1: Capitalism

"Man continually standing in need of the assistance of others, must fall upon some means to procure their help. This he does not merely by coaxing and courting; he does not expect it unless he can turn it to your advantage or make it appear to be so. Mere love is not sufficient for it, till he applies in some way to your self-love. A bargain does this in the easiest manner..."

—Words from the champion of Capitalism,
Adam Smith, in *Lectures on Jurisprudence*, 1896.

Capitalism is defined by Merriam-Webster as an economic system characterized by private or corporate ownership of capital goods, by investments that are determined by private decision, and by prices, production, and the distribution of goods that are determined mainly by competition in a free market.

When it comes to churches, private ownership, profit to the owner, free market, no governmental regulations regarding supply and demand, the market dictates the supply and demand—the result is a mega-church. The typical mega-church is nondenominational, with the senior pastor profiting as owner. There is rarely an overseeing governing body, and the church business caters to "customer" satisfaction. The bottom line is what will bring in the most resources to sustain the enterprise. The churches usually are wonderful edifices, with exceptional facilities, and fabulous shiny brochures. The allure to members is that they get to be counted as members of a thriving ministry, where the pastor may not ever know their names. In fact, a person I know bragged to me about a mega-church he now attends that he has been at the church for seven years and has never met or spoke with the pastor. He liked it that way because in his experience, when the pastor knows him, and finds out that he is a major tither, the relationship changes. (In many mega-churches favoritism is shown to persons with great gifts and large sums of money). The lure then is one of being a part of something great, something rich, something dynamic. Secondly, the lure is that if you ever wanted to start your own business, there is an automatic clientele. Not only can the pastor and key staff make a decent living, you, too, can make a profit by being a part of the church! In fact, many mega-churches have as their vision to build a city within a city. To own apartments, supermarkets, banks, and everything one needs in a model community. This is indeed an attractive lure. On the other hand, the primary agenda of the church can be seen by the public as money-making. It was rumored that my church required a W-2 statement from its members prior to joining. This of course was a ridiculous church myth, related to the lure of capitalism.

Lure # 2: Corporate Structure

Though deservingly criticized, the corporate structure of the church is another lure. The idea that the church is a business, and that that business is winning souls for Christ, frames the controversy. The business of church is often compared to the ministry of church and the two are often in conflict with one another. Yet, people are attracted to the organizational structures, the excellence and efficiency of operations, and the other accoutrements of business life—from the clothes that are worn to the cars that are driven. In his article, "When the Church Becomes a Business", Howey states:

> "Christian church is incorrectly thought of as a place, a service, a building, etc, and not the called out people of God that it really is (the Ecclesia). Most people assume that a church needs to be organized and managed by a CEO (disguised as a shepherd). They end up with a worldly business disguised as a church fully equipped with a worldly military chain-of-command hierarchy (Senior Pastor, Executive Associate Pastor, Associate Pastors, Music Pastor, etc.). This is pure rubbish as it is nowhere to be found in the Bible… "Today 'the church'" jumped out of a van on the way to work to help a little old lady who was shivering in the cold. This is because a Christian jumped out of his van to help that dear woman with her needs and to preach the Gospel to her, showing the love of God in action in tangible reality. This is the church in action." (Howey)

Lure # 3: Recognition of Gifts

Crack addicts are often people with low esteem, lack of confidence, misplaced ambitions, and displaced hopes. Far too often, the very same areas of vulnerability are found in pews. Many hurting people are seeking a place they can "be some-body" and an opportunity to do just that. Especially in the African-American tradition, there was no other place where a person could move from the janitor, cleaning toilets, to the chair of the deacon board, calling the major shots in a congregation. Nowhere could a person who sings in the shower be recognized as the lead vocalist in a choir before hundreds of people. This use of gifts is even more greatly magnified in a mega-church. With health care ministries, counseling ministries, teaching ministries, legal ministries, and teen ministries, to name a few, church-goers could now practice the work they love in the name of ministry and some at the expense of addicts in the pews. The recognition of major gifts in the ministry sells the ministry to the people. There are also detrimental effects. Perceived favoritism based on gifts and income is the primary complaint among persons in the pews and lay leaders. Just as with the first two lures of capitalism and corporate structure, the underside of any lure is a dangerous hook!

Lure #4: Professional Networks

When the average person attends church on a Sunday morning in a mega-church, they assume that the person next to them is there for the same reason; to worship the Lord. Low and behold, a business card is passed to the young man or woman two rows back. A name, phone number, and the business of the month is listed on the card. Smiles are exchanged some professional networking has just transpired.

Because the mega-church attracts the middle to upper middle income crowd, the common man gets to rub shoulders with doctors, lawyers, professional athletes, professors, entrepreneurs, bankers, and building contractors. Every service one may need is "in the house" and the façade is one of equal access—everyone is friendly, everyone is loving, everyone is equal. Or so it appears! For the next two hours, the average parishioner has the pleasure of shaking hands with greatness or rising stars. One member said that it makes her feel hopeful that she too could become a rising star. Yet, these relationships are often superficial and inauthentic, unless the person carries the same amount of professional weight or has something of perceived value to exchange. Some churches even have special networking events, in the name of ministry. Very alluring! The challenge is that not everyone fits in.

Lure #5: Entertainment, Programs, and Productions

Because most mega-churches have large facilities and are maintained by professional staff, they attract major entertainers who are looking to perform for big audiences. In addition, their drama ministries produce the best productions, and their choirs offer the best concerts. Who would not be drawn to join the church where the hub of the community gathers whenever something exciting happens? It becomes the place to be; not only for Saturday night entertainment, but also for Sunday morning worship. Howey believes that such activities are major distractions from the true purpose of ministry. "Theatrical stage shows, pulpit-pew lectures, music concerts and Broadway-like productions passed off as the legitimate activity of real church are ludicrous at best." His premise is that they are there to make money, not to win souls. Be that as it may, many churchgoers are looking for the side attractions and are lured by the entertainment at church, more than they are compelled by the word of the gospel. Thus the question, how was church today is often met with the answer, "Wow! The choir really performed!!"

Lure # 6 Perceived Power

When church leaders appear to be in control of life's challenges— be it family, corporate, or financial matters, this can entice an unsuspecting and basically ignorant seeker. As with the "pusher" who seems to have it all in control, he or she gives directions, and people follow orders. He or she demands services. People hasten to adhere. He or she flaunts money. People are wooed! The same behavior is enticing in the church. In general, there is an innate need to be respected, adored, regarded, and esteemed. So when this is perceived to be available at church, it can be inviting. "I want that same power!" "I need that same respect!" In fact, historically, this has been the lure of African-American churches. Because there was no power to be found in the world for an oppressed people, status and power were sought after in the church. There is nothing wrong with genuine influence that is for positive results, but as we all know: "All that glitters ain't gold!" When the power of deception is at work, the seeds of darkness are present and often take root in the lives of innocent people. This is a dangerous lure!

Genuine Fellowship (Countering the Bait)

While the bait is enticing, none of the professionals in the pews, outstanding musicians, or dynamic expositors in the pulpit, can replace the need for genuine Christian fellowship. People leave productions unchanged. They are lulled for the moment into forgetting life issues. They laugh and cry, shout and sing, high five their neighbors and greet in Jesus' name, only to leave the place designed for worship and fellowship, alone and dejected. What is needed are intimate authentic encounters with other believers and what is often experienced is bleacher-behavior—strangers rooting for the same team, cheering for the same performances, never really knowing each other or addressing the reason for being at church. What can we do about it? Here are five things that may counter the bait:

1. Opportunities to get to know the pastor and lay leaders personally, besides the common "scheduled" fellowships. Jesus called the twelve "to Himself" meaning He was relational with his disciples. Too many pastors and church leaders are seen as "untouchable."

2. Opportunities to be a part of a small prayer group, bible study, or fellowship group which meet the direct needs of the people and foster real relationships.

3. Opportunities to ask questions and receive answers regarding fiscal accountability without insult or injury!

4. Messages about Godly priorities and balance from the pulpit, accompanied by the modeling of "first families". Leadership should never teach what it refuses to practice!

5. Healthy respect for families and sensitivity to demands for time, talents and treasures.

Reflection Questions:

1. Do I know enough about the church I attend and its leaders to follow its teachings and leadership?

2. Am I emotionally drawn to my church to satisfy or deny a deeper need that I have neglected to face?

CHAPTER THREE

I'M HOOKED
(UNDERSTANDING DEPENDENCY IN THE CHURCH)

"Cursed is the one who trusts in man, who depends on flesh for his strength and whose heart turns away from the LORD." (Jeremiah17: 5)

Jeremiah cautions Israel not to rely on false gods and unhealthy alliances for their well-being. This type of trust invariably turns a righteous person away from God. As we mature in faith, we begin to clearly distinguish the enormity of the God we serve and by contrast, the ineptness of many of His representatives.

The preference of corruptible men to God invokes curse and damnation. The Lord is appalled at the thought of mortal men finding strength in the heart of another man, at the expense of relationship with Him. While scripture encourages us to find strength in our fellow man, the Lord warns of dependence on another man for what only He can provide. When earthly relationships foster private dependencies that cause one to rely solely on another, which causes the heart to turn away from God, The Lord has been violated!

Every addict must have an idol that serves as the focus of its addiction says Melodie Beattie (1987), author of *Codependent No More*. People from all walks of life, especially those who profess to have a personal relationship with Jesus Christ, would love to think they totally depend upon God. These same people might also believe that dependency is some complicated malady that affects others, and the words "I'm hooked" could never be mentioned in a sentence that also bears their name. Not only is it possible to be hooked on a substance such as crack cocaine, but we might be hooked on the church. What many of us need, however, is a clear, concise understanding of dependency and how dependency is an issue in the church.

Dependency is often used interchangeably with the word addiction. Physiologically, dependence has two symptoms, withdrawal when the drug is taken away, and tolerance, which means that more and more of the same drug is needed to achieve the original effect. (Narconon International)

Awakened to realize they're in a different grip and it's not grace, the life of a crack addict is replete with stories of deeper and greater dependency, ending in bondage to a chemical that has insidiously and gradually become the power and authority over their life. The initial experience with crack leads to continued use, accompanied by the rapid development of tolerance.

Tolerance is a dangerous place of adaptation, made worse by the silent reality of a seemingly insatiable monster within, that always demands more where less used to be enough. The addict has little choice but to live in a state of denial in order to survive the chokehold of the rock. This facilitates a slow but assured death, and not just from the toxicity of the drug. Whether spiritual, physical, emotional or relational, the death often includes the ambush of a mind that loses its ability to make conscious choices based upon firm realities. Thus, the addict creates his own reality.

Like crack addiction, far too often innocent parishioners are influenced so heavily by church leaders that they find themselves in a state of what I call "tolerant acceptance". Church leadership requires more and more of time, money, performance of duties, for the same or less compensation, and little or no expressed gratitude. Addicts continue to seek approval and will do more and more to get the desired acknowledgment.

Just as with the life of the crack addict, as the addict "comes down" in a sober moment, they will quickly tell you that they are sick of their lifestyle yet are confined to the grip. Those who practice tolerant acceptance are no different. If given the opportunity they will quickly confess to the ills of the church and the underside of the bait or lure, but for some reason, continue to tolerate it. They are hooked!

Psychologically, dependence is the sense of needing or craving the substance. Socially, the substance is continued in spite of the cost to other areas of life (work life, home life, family relationships, friendships, and finances).

According to Ms. M, she realized that she was hooked when she started stealing from her family:

"I knew I was addicted when I started taking from my family, my grandchildren, my mother, my children, whoever. It's a sad thing when you steal from your family. I took from my family because I had this attitude that if I take from them they are not going to hurt me."

Ms. M realized that her family loved her enough not to turn her in if she stole from them. Ironically, those she loved most became the same ones she neglected and took advantage of. She had a new allegiance. When asked why she continued to use or what kept her hooked, Ms. M referred to her own sense of isolation from the very family she stole from. The isolation seemed so painful that the only thing she knew to alleviate the pain was more crack. Crack was the source of her pain, but it was also the cure for her pain. She was hooked.

How does one know when they are hooked on the church? Many find the same relief as David did when he exclaimed, I was glad when they said unto me let us go into the house of the Lord! Is this addiction to the church negative and something to be feared? Or like David, does it speak to the preeminence of God in your life? Interestingly enough, one might use the same litmus test as addiction to drugs. Does the absence of church cause significant behavior change? For example, does your behavior shift to its pre-saved state? Do your positive emotions depend on whether or not you made it to the sanctuary? More importantly, is there any consequence to your work life, your family life, and your important relationships as a result of your church involvement? Has the very thing you love about church also been the source of great pain? Have you been accused of or made to feel that the church could open or close without your presence? Was it true???

I knew that I was becoming addicted to the church when the church became a priority above everything else in my life, including my family, special occasions that I (in the past) never missed, never would avoid missing; never would allow anything to get in front of it. The church at that time in my life was the place where I did everything; and there's nothing wrong with that. There's nothing wrong with the church providing a holistic approach to ministry. But, in my case, if I could not be at the church, I was not strong in any other setting. The church provided for me a kind of covering. It protected me from some unpleasant stuff; for example, in my family there were some strained relationships. So, I could use the church (because the church always had something going on) as an excuse for not making some family functions. I could use the church to get off from work, and because the church always had something going on, I felt that every time the church doors were opened, I was supposed to be there.

Being a young mother, my life was becoming grossly imbalanced, but at the time it seemed that the church answered every question for my life that I had. Even down to raising my children. The children were in the church school. The children I taught were at the church school. So, I began to realize that I had somewhat of an organizational addiction when every question in my life was answered by the church.

What kept me in that addicted state was the fact that there were several people around me who experienced and enjoyed the exact same abnormalities. We never had conversations, for example, about balance, our families, visiting with family and ensuring that those primary relationships were solid and secure and blessed. It was, therefore, easy for me to use the church as a scapegoat because the church provided what I thought was everything that I needed. So, nobody was going to tell me that there was anything wrong with being in church 24 hours a day/seven days a week. That's what I thought; that's what I lived by and I became addicted to the organization. I was addicted to all of the many ministries. It was popular; it was moving quickly. It was the fastest-growing ministry in the city that I live in, and to be attached to that was just exciting to me. Was I being healed at that time, was I be delivered at that time—that's another question—but I was having fun. Fun to me was all that mattered. Nobody questioned me about what I did when I left church—there was not private accountability for my life. When I left church, they would see me the next day— as was the case for over a thousand other people. So, we all sort of floated in and out—disconnected in any real sense, yet connected through a false sense of security and loyalty. That's when I recognized that I was addicted, and what kept me addicted was the recognition that there were so many other respectable people in the same boat. None of us were really bothering each other, so we were able to co-habit a culture that had been created for silence. That's what gave me my strength, and I supported others in their addiction as well, as they supported me. "Come on girl and go to the banquet with me!" But, they'd say, "My husband isn't in the church!" "O, he'll be alright, he'll get over it!! You live your life in front of him, he'll come on board!" We spoke those kinds of brash comments back to people in support of their addiction as well. So, quickly I began to see that all of us were united in this front of happiness—that's what the surface looked like, but in the chapters that follow, we'll talk about what was really going on underneath.

Another important concept in our discussion at this point is the concept of co-dependence. I alluded to it when I shared that at times we encouraged each other in our addictions. When a person who is not yet an addict supports someone else in their addictions, we used words like enabling. An enabler makes it easier for someone to remain addicted...they support, encourage, cover, make excuses for, permit, allow, and publicly defend the addict at all costs. In fact, one might say that they are addicted to the addict. Addiction to the addict is how social scientists define co-dependence in simple terms. It would be easy to see how entire congregations of churches might support the culture of co-dependent leaders, lay ministers, and other members. That's a lot of support to continue an addiction.

To complicate the organizational dynamic further, there are times when the pusher is also an addict. On the streets, if the pusher is his own number one customer, he will soon be out of business. He must not use the same substances he or she pushes or must only use from his excess. If the pusher is in the pulpit, his or her addiction may be to pure cocaine compared to the addict in the pew who is addicted to crack.

In other words, what happens to congregants when the pusher in the pulpit is "addicted" to his or her own issues, be they issues of high need for achievement, the need for place of excitement to assuage the pains of life, or the tri-fold issues of power, control, and domination? If the positive reinforcements of being in their positions are alluring enough, they risk becoming addicted. From the seat of the addict in the pew, the person in the pulpit looks alluring. He or she has charisma, superficial charm, confident spirituality, and connections with important people. Additionally, they are articulate, world travelers, sharp dressers—alluring enough to form dangerous alliances with. Not only is the unsuspecting congregant hooked by the bait, but also hooked on the pusher. Again, this type of addiction is known as co-dependence and is rampant in the church.

The National Institute on Drug Abuse, in a publication on the treatment of cocaine addiction, gives the following definition of co-dependency:

> "Co-dependents become co-dependent because they have learned to believe that love, acceptance, security, and approval are contingent upon taking care of the addict in the way the addict wishes. In their decision-making process, they allow the addict to define reality. Unfortunately, this excessive care-giving behavior tends to foster even more dependency on the part of the addict." (http://www.drugabuse.gov/TXManuals/IDCA/IDCA11.html)

Consider the above definition, while picturing the average pastor as the addict. The church makes no apologies in its biblical teaching of caring for the pastor. A pastor that labors in the word and teaching is worthy of double honor (1 Timothy 5:17). However, no pastor or other human being for that matter should be able to affect or control one's sense of self-worth and self-definition. The unhealthy dependence on any external sources is complicated by unhealed emotions from childhood, which causes the co-dependent to relinquish power and self-esteem when familiar emotions are pricked. This is a dangerous proposition for those responsible for caring for the souls of the persons assigned to them (Beattie, 1987). As it pertains to the crack cocaine addict, authority is abdicated to the drug and the source of the supply. As it pertains to the church, the throne of sick, unhealed, narcissistic church leaders is heightened.

Many people suffering from co-dependency grow up in homes where there is alcoholism or drug addiction, particularly on the part of the parents, so they think it's normal to live with someone who is abusive, neglectful and needs to be taken care of all the time. Ms. M grew up watching an older brother's addiction to heroine. He would warn her not to get involved with drugs, she watched him and challenged him that he could not tell her how to live, if he was not willing to live by the same standards. Ms. M's brother was killed in the prime of his life—a drug-related death.

People with co-dependency lose their independence and frequently become more concerned about the addict's life more than their own. They also tend to be perfectionists and overly-responsible—afraid to disappoint the addict or fail to protect the family's reputation. And like people who are addicted, the vast majority of people suffering from co-dependency never recognize their co-dependency until a crisis occurs. (For more information on co-dependency, see, "Addiction and Co-Dependency"—West Penn Allegheny Health System.)

Friel & Subby (1984) list the rules that keep us stuck in a co-dependent pattern of living and are strikingly identical to the co-dependence experienced in most churches today. I have modified these somewhat to integrate them with my own experiences of co-dependent relationships in church:

1. It is not okay to talk about problems, and feelings should not be openly expressed—the culture of silence is reinforced.

2. Communication is best if indirect, with one person acting as messenger between two others—triangulation is a preferred mode of communication.

3. The leaders must be protected at all costs, even if it means misrepresenting the truth or the facts—loyalty is demanded, even if it is false (non-genuine) loyalty.

4. Good effort without results means little—perfection (not excellence) appears to be the unspoken goal.

5. Discipline must be exacted on the entire group when things go wrong—a shotgun vs. rifle approach is used, so that all feel guilty and responsible for whatever goes wrong.

These rules all seem to be designed to protect the status quo of the organizations and to protect the leader at all costs. These are the characteristics of a dysfunctional family as well as a dysfunctional church. Ironically, most highly functioning people miraculously come forth in spite of so called dysfunctional upbringings. I agree with others who attest that the best and the worst of themselves came from the ashes of dysfunction. Such can also be said about my experience with the church. If any of these rules appear to be ones that are operative in your church pray for discernment—you may be in a co-dependent church.

> "Much of recovery is finding and maintaining balance in all areas of our lives. We need to watch the scales so they do not tip too far to either side as we measure our responsibilities to ourselves and to others. We need to balance our emotional needs with our physical, mental, and spiritual needs. We need to balance giving and receiving; we need to find the dividing line between letting go and doing our part." (Beattie, p. 211)

To understand the process of addiction, consider the law of supply and demand. There is a need that creates a demand. The need may be a pre-existing emotional state, resulting from depression, despair, discouragement, disorientation or any type of a void waiting to be filled. Because of the need, there is an openness, a vulnerability and willingness to trust others to inform and impact your life. The entrusted one, the supplier, purports to have what you need, and declares that it is to be met with your best interest at heart. There is an exchange—something you give, expecting to be supplied as promised. There is a gradual demand for more than you bargained for to keep the same level of peace, and a strange sense of belonging…"I'm in the place designed to meet my needs." The problem is that the supplier raises the ante; it costs more and more to achieve the same level of satisfaction—you can never pay enough or receive enough… before you know it, you are an addict in the pew!

Reflection Questions:

I lived dependent upon man's assessment of my future, my family, my faith and my finances for almost 20 years. Afraid to enter a territory beyond human dependency, I found a way to survive, without my own origin of thought, without knowledge of the pitfalls that accompany addiction, with absolutely no idea of the journey to recovery. Wow, as smart, gifted and discerning as I am, I never would have thought I was an addict in the pew! Are you an addict in the pew? Ask yourself these questions.

1. Do I allow church attendance and activity to fill a need such as loneliness, depression, despair, rather than facing my own needs?

2. Are there personalities in leadership that I have secretly attached myself to, and really do not feel as if my week is complete unless I touch base with them?

3. Is the pastor of my church someone that I trust to make me feel better each week? Or is it my communion with God that makes me feel better?

4. If not in church, am I able to connect with God in the same way?

CHAPTER FOUR

IT BECAME MY GOD
(UNDERSTANDING IDOLATRY IN THE CHURCH)

"And He said to me, "Son of man, do you see what they are doing?—the utterly detestable things the house of Israel is doing here, things that will drive me far from my sanctuary?...Then He brought me to the entrance of the court. I looked, and I saw a hole in the wall. He said to me, Son of man, now dig into the wall. So I dug into the wall and saw a doorway there. And He said to me, "Go in and see the wicked and detestable things they are doing here." So I went in and looked, and I saw portrayed all over the walls all kinds of crawling things and detestable animals and all the idols of the house of Israel. In front of them stood seventy elders of the house of Israel...Each had a censer in his hand, and a fragrant cloud of incense was rising. He said to me, "Son of man, have you seen what the elders of the house of Israel are doing in the darkness, each at the shrine of his own idol? They say, The Lord does not see us; the Lord has forsaken the land."
(Ezekiel 8: 6-12)

The book of Ezekiel is a prophetic book of the Old Testament with vivid, symbolic language. Having lived among the other citizens of the nation of Judah as a Babylonian captive himself, Ezekiel began to receive his prophetic messages from God and was instructed to address these prophecies to the Jews who were also in captivity. In one such message, he describes God's judgment on the nation of Judah because of its rampant idolatry.

Through the revelation experience of Ezekiel, we see the very essence of deception and idolatry. Orton (2004) describes it as "Snakes in the Temple".

Hidden deep within the walls of the temple, in a dark and secret room, the elders worshipped false images. The King James Bible describes the room as the chamber of his own imagery. Every home at this time had a room or a closet dedicated to the secret worship of images. This room in the temple was so secret though, that the prophet was instructed to dig through a small hole in the wall to discover it.

Inside the room, Ezekiel saw images of crawling things covering the walls, detestable animals and all the idols of Israel. The Hebrew term for "crawling things" (remes) refers to all small animals such as rodents and especially reptiles. Ezekiel saw, among other creatures, snakes on the wall of this hidden room.

Though what Ezekiel saw was hidden, it was blatant rejection of the Lord's covenant which prohibited idolatry of "creatures that move along the ground" (Deuteronomy 4: 15-18). This text uses the noun form of "crawling things" which also carries the meaning of animals that glide along the ground—i.e. snakes, although the worship of snakes and other creatures was, in fact, an out-and-out rejection of the Lord's covenant love.

However, despite the hidden practice of snake worship on the inside, from the outside nothing had changed. The *temple looked the same*. To the naked eye, it was still the Holy place of God's presence. This is the very essence of deception—an external appearance of spirituality, but an altogether different reality from within!

I have often felt that I could relate to the prophet Ezekiel. Having lived among the "captives" myself, I knew of the private practices and deception among the ranks of the "elite". When God called me, He too began to speak and to show me things privately, often through the use of visions. I used to sit in worship as a participant, with my mind racing with questions and observations. I sought the Lord for answers and understanding. When He began to reveal, I was startled. I used to beg God, "Stop! I don't want to know anymore! I don't want to see anymore! I don't want to hear anymore!" But just as Ezekiel, based upon internal evidence from the Lord, I would become a spokesman called by and for Him, declaring the revelation, pronouncing the judgment and proclaiming the future restoration of the people.

> "And what agreement hath the temple of God with idols? For ye are the temple of the living God; as God hath said, I will dwell in them, and walk in them; and I will be their God, and they shall be my people. Wherefore come out from among them, and be ye separate, saith the Lord, and touch not the unclean thing; and I will receive you." 2 Corinthians 6:16-17

Anything and anybody that becomes more important in your life than God, is an idol. God is jealous and has righteous anger against any form of idolatry.

"You shall not make for yourself an idol, or any likeness of what is in heaven above or on the earth beneath or in the water under the earth. You shall not worship them or serve them; for I, the Lord your God, am a jealous God, visiting the iniquity of the fathers on the children, on the third and fourth generations of those who hate Me, but showing loving kindness to thousands, to those who love Me and keep My commandments." (Exodus 20:4-6)

Why should God, the Creator of all living things, play second fiddle to something that His creation (man) creates (wood carving) as a representation of Him (almighty God). Man, who was given dominion over all of creation, finds a portion of what he has dominion over, a piece of wood, or gold, and carves out an image to worship. It literally reverses the order of creation as God intended. Isn't it easy to see why God detests idol worship? Rather than lifting up the God of all creation, the creature serves the very thing he is to have dominion over. God hates idols, it doesn't matter if it is the image of the sun or the moon, the fish god, the fertility goddess, golf, sports, clothes, cars, titles, sex, or drugs—whatever takes the place of centrality on the throne other than God Almighty, is an idol, and God hates it.

The Lord is appalled at the very idea of a life lived without Him as center. When the very nucleus of our existence is occupied by anything or anyone other than Himself, the remainder of our world becomes a misrepresentation of who we were created to be and misguided as to what we were created to do. I realized something a few years ago regarding a misrepresented nucleus, and it represents why many refuse to let go of the idol…that is this: anytime you give an uncompromised yes to God, you will cause inconvenience to the idol! It can be scary, it can cause rejections, and it will certainly call for a realignment of one's life.

An addict has usually elevated his or her drug of choice to a central place in his or her life and all of the rest of life revolves around this center. What does the crack addict think of as soon as they open their eyes from slumber—the next hit and the supplier. It is not uncommon for crack addicts to brag about the level of high attained with the dope from a given dealer. They ascribe worth to the drug as if it has god-like qualities. The crack addict has an insatiable desire to be in the presence of his crack. It, in fact, becomes his or her master and there is very little the addict won't do for the god, crack. Who or what a person worships, he or she will also serve. God is jealous. It hurts His heart when we serve the created over the creator. Yes it does.

Despite the debilitating effects of crack cocaine upon the user, somehow the dependency becomes so great that the drug takes over as the top priority in the life of the user. Interviews with many families of addicts reveal consistently the outrage of theft, lies, and trickery used against the innocent for the purpose of feeding this sense of hopelessness and underlying unhappiness. Such was the case with Ms. M. Crack had become the thing she lived for, the thing that shaped her values, changed her mood, and satisfied her heart's desire. Crack cocaine can take preeminence in the life of its users and so can church! It becomes an idol, a god with a little "g". In fact, in his article, "Addiction and Grace", Gerald May writes that addiction is the most powerful psychic enemy of humanity's desire for God.

As with other addictions, it appears that there is a spiritual longing. I heard someone describe it as a vacuum shaped only for God that drugs, sex, food, drink, people, money, achievement, or success cannot fill. When a soul aches to be healed, it longs for God. When God seems absent, it reaches for a temporary fix. Like the men of Judah in Ezekiel's vision, we do our private idol worship deep within the walls and confines of our secret places.

The Bible clearly says that "God is a jealous God, and thou shall have no other gods before me." I realized that the church had become priority in my life, and let me preface this by saying that the church *is* a priority in my life, but it's not the top priority—that's not the order that God set up. But, at that time in my life, the church was first, and was even before God. I realized the church had become an idol in my life whenever God would say for me to do things and they would seem contradictory to what the church was asking me to do. Although I was still healing at the time, I had been in church all my life (and though I had many questions in my life and for my life) I knew how to do church and never had a question about hearing the voice of God. But, when the Lord would speak to me and give me directives for my life, it was as though I would ignore them if they were contradictory to my schedule at the church. That's when I realized that the church was becoming a priority in my life and that my pastor was becoming an idol. There's nothing wrong with loving your pastor or respecting your pastor, but there is a difference in building healthy spiritual relationships and building relationships that eventually will lead to some form of co-dependence or emotional attachments that are unhealthy or do not allow for an individual to grow in God. I began to realize this when my pastor became an idol. Everything that he wanted, I wanted to make sure that if I was a part of it, he was going to get it. There's nothing wrong with this, given the proper context of the church and structure of the church. But, when the priority becomes not pleasing to God, but pleasing to man, then there's idolatry and there's a problem.

I realized this about mid-way through my journey at that church when the Lord began to tell me to do things, and when I began to do them, I would run into opposition from the church. That's when I recognized—hmmm something is going on here that's not quite right. I was continuing still to have a great time, a wonderful time in the church. I was at the church 24 hours a day not understanding what was going on inside me...

I then began to think about the church and how it origi-nated and began to study the Bible and recognized that the family was ordained in the Book of Genesis, but the church does not come about until the Book of Acts. God lines up our priorities where He's first and then the family and then the church …That's when I realized that the priority of the church was simply out of order in the church I attended.

There was daily evidence, reflected in my life at the time that helped me to know that I had improperly prioritized things: I put the church before my family. When one puts the church before one's family, something is wrong. Therefore, it is my heart's desire even now in ministry never to allow that to happen with young families that come behind me. There are several reasons for that. First, most husbands will not say anything to a wife about the church because the church is such a sacred place. It is such the place that one always expects is honorable and that all is well and how dare they ever say anything negative or derogatory about the church. So, many marriages are busting up with people in the church with misguided priorities because they can't be honest regarding the time they spend at church.

My case was no different. I thought that I was doing what the Lord wanted me to do—how could I be wrong being in the church 24/seven? How could I be wrong? But I realized that my husband never questioned me about that and sat silently by (he, by the way, was also in the church). Instead, he watched my issues and ethics being practiced in two different ways—one in the church and one in the home. Yet, he would never ask me anything about my obligation to the church nor put his foot down regarding any obligation to the church primarily because the church is the place one never questions.

I think it's important to note that when a culture of silence has been created regarding the church and how it practices church (if you will), then you have a culture of silence that's not only created in the congregation, but it filters over and becomes created in the homes. Then we have congregations full of unhealthy families who are not conversing because we don't speak openly about these issues in the church and we certainly won't do it at home. So, I think it's necessary to note regarding the idolatry that the church can become involved in.

I note here that most addicts do more than misappropriate priorities. They steal and compromise their morality to support their habits. So I ask myself the question, "Did I ever steal to support my habit?" I think it is critical to note that when a family is not on the same page and of one accord regarding finances, and one is spending every penny they have in the church and the other one is just silently sitting by, as a wife, I believe now in retrospect, that I should have been of one accord with my husband as to how we managed our finances and how we did all those things. Although I was doing it biblically and according to the word of the Lord, the question is was I always in communication with my husband? No! Was I in the practice of seeking him and his covering and counsel when writing checks above and beyond my tithe and offering and with regard to sacrificial giving (which I believe in)? No!

I want to emphasize here, it is important for families to be of one accord in all these areas. It's the same as feeling as if you have to hide your purchases from your spouse in the trunk of your car after going shopping. When this is the case, there are issues of mistrust and dishonesty that begin to prevail in the relationship and, again, because of the silent culture where certain things not talked about, we are not only wreaking havoc in the church, but, like termites tearing at the walls, we have let that demon infest our homes.

Do you call this stealing? Perhaps not, but if it's a half truth, it's a whole lie. I believe we have many people who manage their finances in half-truths in the kingdom and I don't think that's healthy. Please also note that giving the tithe and offering has never been an option in my life. This was never up for discussion and is not a Christian's option. However, giving of my time, talent and treasures in other areas is something that needs to be discussed with my spouse and the same is true for anyone else who is married and certainly for those of us who call ourselves Christians. This should be collaborated upon so that balance is assured, even if it is not directed from the church. Somebody in the family should be emotionally strong enough and desirous of a healthy relationship such that those kinds of dialogues are frequent and they are constant and they are always honest.

How then can we prevent church life or people in the church from becoming our idols? Let's look to the Word for answers.

> [21]*For although they knew God, they neither glorified him as God nor gave thanks to him, but their thinking became futile and their foolish hearts were darkened.* [22]*Although they claimed to be wise, they became fools* [23]*and exchanged the glory of the immortal God for images made to look like mortal man and birds and animals and reptiles.* (Romans 8:21-23,NIV)

From this passage, the answer seems apparent; glorify God! Give thanks to Him always. Make Him your ultimate priority. Examine the priorities in your life. Keep God first, and note what comes second, third, fourth, etc. Is it your spouse, your children, your job, your ministry, the church? Study the Word of God to see the value of these and prioritize accordingly. Then and only then will you rid yourself of snakes in the temple and other little g gods.

Reflection Questions:

Beloved, we must choose to center our affections on Jesus, to root ourselves in His word and to drive any and all misrepresentations of Him out of our lives. The choice to live for God and not man can be painful but Christ warned us of that. The choice to remove false gods can seem lonely, but Christ prepared us for that. The decision to make Him your God and declare none before Him can feel disloyal, but Christ has exposed the deception in that. The commitment to serve Him according to His will, His ways and His word can seem demanding, but be encouraged; Christ has already paid for that.

Do you have any false gods that compete with your loyalty to the true and living God?

Are you fully committed to serving Him according to His will and His way?

CHAPTER FIVE

LIVING APART FROM REALITY
(A DISTORTED CHRISTIANITY)

"Have nothing to do with the fruitless deeds of darkness, but rather expose them." (Ephesians 5:11, NIV)

Paul exhorts the believer to always be truthful and take a stand for that which is right. So often in the life of the church, the believer is challenged with this question: should I do what is right or should I go along to keep peace? (A false sense of peace, I might add.) This dilemma of going along to keep the peace should never serve as a guiding factor for a Christian's conduct. The scriptures clearly teach us how we are to walk, how we are to live, how we are to love and how we are to obey. One must always be mindful of this reality....silence can be interpreted as approval!

The travesty in today's society is that many who discern wickedness, trickery and darkness, especially in the church, are afraid to confront it! For fear of being ostracized or rejected, many recognize the opposition but rarely if ever expose it. Thus, we have learned to accept it. We have learned how to live with it and have mastered how to cover it up. Our skills have become intrinsically embedded so much so, that we accept as right that which we know to be wrong, we accept as pure that which we know to be filthy, and we accept as truth that which we know to be a lie. Deception from the father of lies has won—even in the church!!! It has all but paralyzed truth and has silenced any confession of sin. Wow, and isn't that exactly what addictions do? And to think that even professing Christians can become victims of internal addictions, affected heavily by the idols of their affections, so much so that our very doctrine can so easily be compromised. Solomon in Proverbs 16:25 said it like this:

> *There is a way that seemeth right unto a man, but the end thereof are the ways of death.* (Proverbs 16:25)

There is a way of life that may seem harmless, when in fact it produces sheer destruction and death. The addict finds him or herself living a life that is desperately different from any lifestyle he or she could think or imagine, but somehow, deludes him or herself into believing that all is well. Denial is an addict's worse enemy. It is a fundamental departure from reality whereby the person engaging in it is the last to know. It is a psychological defense mechanism which allows a person to ignore, rationalize or push past facts in order to construct a more acceptable reality. It blocks hope, progress, and change. This enemy not only robs one of all hope of recovery, but soothes the ego, satisfies the heart, and justifies the untoward behavior.

The Encyclopedia of Mental Disorders defines denial as "the refusal to acknowledge the existence or severity of unpleasant external realities or internal thoughts and feelings".

The first step in any recovery program is to address the issue of denial. I am an addict, but I still love the Lord. (If you love him you would obey his commandments—thou shall have no other gods before me, Exodus 34:14). I am an addict but I still am an honest person. (If you are honest, why do you lie or embellish the truth to get money to support your habit?) I am not really an addict; I could stop anytime I want to. Why did you just spend two hundred dollars on drugs when you don't have any food in your cupboards to feed your family? It would seem to me that you'd want to stop after repeated assaults, some sexual, loss of friends, property, self-respect. Perhaps you are living a different reality than you are willing to admit.

In Ms. M's eyes at that time, because crack was seemingly satisfying her emptiness, loneliness, rejection, and because it was thought to be satisfying a need in her that only God could fill, she rationalized that God must have sent the drug to her. There were times she didn't know where her next hit was coming from and right in the middle of crashing, God would send her someone to exchange favors for drugs. This was distorted thinking to say the least. God has nothing to do with your destruction.

Another radical departure from reality occurs when the addict engages in escapism. Note John Wesley's thoughts in a recent article published October, 2007, "Overcoming Addictions and Escapism", and the parallel to the addictions we find in the pews as parishioners seek to "escape reality". John Wesley says it best:

"Everyone feels the desire to escape. No matter how good you have it, there are times when, instead of dealing with problems, you'd rather pretend they don't exist. We turn to bad habits because they allow us to forget. They give us a pleasurable sensation that pushes problems out of mind. The downfall of this solution is that it's only temporary. The feeling wears off and the problems remain, often made worse by our indulgence. Once again faced with our problems, the natural reaction is to escape again. This is the cycle of escapism. We feel pain each time we face reality, so we use a bad habit to escape, which only increases our pain, making us more desperate to escape. Each time around it takes more sensation to escape, increasing our dependency on a bad habit. When you get caught in the whirlpool of escapism, it can feel impossible to get out."

Denial and escapism are alive and well in the church. Church folk often create a separate reality from those around them, especially if they are addicts. The "way that seems right" to addicts in the pews and other devoted Christians, is usually not an obvious departure like getting high on drugs every day. However, the subtlety of calling wrong right also leads to death and destruction. In church it may take the form of hypocrisy or being "blind guides." (You blind guides! You strain out a gnat but swallow a camel. Matthew 23:24) Outwardly, the behavior looks fine to world, but the inner life is ruinous, filled with pride, self-aggrandizement, self-conceit, and self-righteousness. The way of *self-righteousness* seems right unto man but leads to death.

From my perspective at the time, I saw anyone who was not doing what I was doing (and this is self-righteousness at its best) as being wrong. If anyone in my family did not have affiliation with a church that they were involved in at least five of seven days a week, I felt they were missing something, they were wrong and somewhere in their lives they had failed God. It was a reality of mine that this was the way life is supposed to be lived, and therefore I saw nothing about my way of thinking as wrong. Furthermore, I saw everybody who did not think as I did as being wrong. Even other members who would come to the church faithfully were judged by me and those who supported my addiction because they had like additions. We used to actually judge their commitment based upon our standards. If they were not doing what we were doing, we would ostracize them from leadership, put them down, suggest they were not believers, didn't love God, were confused about their salvation, and all those kinds of incorrect assessments. This was the life we were living and the judgmental spirit under which we were operating. I found that that reality was so distorted—it was such a distorted Christianity based upon the needs of people and not the sound directives of God. I began to realize that I was living apart from reality, and if anybody questioned (including my own mother who used to speak of our constant participation at the church—not our relationship with God, but our constant need to be so tied to the church) I would deny the stronghold that had me so attached to the church because, again, all of the things in my life that I thought needed answering were (I thought) being answered.

Everything at the time that I needed from a standpoint of socialization, emotional attachments—church was high, the choir was good, it felt good for about an hour and a half—then I went right back into my traps and back into my own dysfunction. But at the time it served what I needed and nobody, not anybody—including my mother—was going to make me see that there was anything wrong with what I was doing. Was I living in denial? I now know that I was. But, at the time, again I think it's important to note, that distortion and living apart from reality come whenever you are determined to believe that there's nothing wrong.

There were some things that I thought were so real— I thought fellowship was real and I later found out that it was mandated and legislated. I thought that this thing that I called fun was so real until I began to meet the others who were around me (and in their addiction as well) realize from a truth standpoint that this was a major, major forest of deception. I thought that love was real until I needed it and didn't get it. I thought that friendship was real until I needed it and didn't get it. I really thought that mentoring was real until I started growing and my growth was cursed. I really thought that learning the Bible and application of the Word was real. I thought that that teaching was real until I began to apply it. As soon as I began responding to God and not responding to people, rejection came in waves of heaviness. When I began to ask for the assistance that friends ask for from one another, I found instead backbiting and my assistance no longer needed. I just could not believe that the same people who said they loved me so much could cut me off and be through with me in a matter of seconds. I was beginning to see that so many things that I thought were real simply were not.

At that point, I made a conscious decision within, even as I was still there serving and doing everything I was called and asked to do, to shift from pleasing man to pleasing God. As I made this decision, I began to ask myself, apart from what was being taught about God and church, what was the Lord saying to His Minister. By then, I had accepted my call not just to preach, but to pastor. I asked myself, what the Lord would require of me, if I were in the position of pastor. The Lord impressed upon me that there would be three areas to guard:

1. His People—they must never be emotionally manipulated for the sake of the church.

2. His Word—it must never be distorted, diminished, or embellished for the sake of the church.

3. His Church—she must never be held hostage to legalism at the expense of freedom in Christ.

When any of these areas became tools for enabling unhealthy addictions, I was to call them what they are: witchcraft, sorcery, divination, manipulation, demonic influence, and control—tactics that do not originate from Him, but from the enemy; and strategies that are as destructive as giving a hurting person a quick hit of crack cocaine to alleviate their pain. Or worse, as despicable as pushing my own agenda to support my own needs over the needs of God's elect. I believe God would view ALL of these as abominations.

Honestly, even as my eyes were opening to the pitfalls of pastoring, I still enabled the ungodly tactics of leadership at times. I enabled them most of the time, with silence and dutiful compliance, indicating to others, I know, I see, and I support. My rationalization was: this is not your flock, you are here to be an obedient servant, you are employed, do your job. God forgive me if I have furthered the addictions of others.

It is indeed my hope that all who are called to pastor would form a common bond around these three areas of caution. I pray that all would be equally committed to the people, the word, and the church. That all would examine themselves prayerfully in the face of almighty God and ask the question: am I pushing dope or hope? Is my reality distorted? The next three chapters hit hard. They are not intended to judge but to inform and convict if necessary. I hold myself to the standards presented here. I trust that they will serve as precautionary guides for your life as you become gatekeepers to prevent spiritual abuse in the pulpit and in the pews.

If you are a pastor, I challenge you to pray this prayer before reading the next chapters:

> Lord, open my eyes so that I might embrace the reality of my calling. I am in a position to influence others. Let me never compromise your trust in me, by manipulating your people, your word, or your church. Let me not engage in manipulation, but in truth and in love. Help me to be a good shepherd, leading as you lead, loving as you love. Amen.

CHAPTER SIX

THE POWER OF CHARISMATIC INFLUENCE
(EMOTIONAL MANIPULATION)

"Every plant that my heavenly Father has not planted will be pulled up by the roots. Leave them; they are blind guides. If a blind man leads a blind man, both will fall into a pit." (Matthew 15:13-14, NIV)

Jesus told His disciples to leave the Pharisees alone because the Pharisees were blind to God's truth. To be considered blind to God's truth is not to be ignorant of God's truth. The Pharisees knew the Word of God! Being blind to God's truth is the willful and concrete decision to not apply God's truth. It is to operate with a reprobate mind. It is to ignore truth as it pertains to oneself. It is the skillful and tactful presentation of truth to others with the intentional exemption of oneself. This is blindness to God's truth. Jesus was warning that anyone who listened to their teaching would risk spiritual blindness as well. Not all religious leaders clearly see or accept God's truth. Many spiritual leaders refuse to follow the principles of scripture and are adamant about their own perceived authority.

A blind guide here is contrasted to a plant not planted by God. As a result, it is not expected to bear the fruit of His spirit. As such, a leader not called by God, relying on his or her charismatic influence to falsely guide innocent followers down paths of personal destruction, is a blind guide. We are warned to leave them, before we all fall into the same pit.

Charisma, from the Greek word for gift, is a personality trait characterized by a certain kind of magical charm that arouses loyalty and enthusiasm, especially toward leaders. To manipulate is to control or play upon by artful, unfair, or insidious means for the sole purpose of working to one's own advantage. It is the ability to "handle" with great skill. (Definitions were obtained from Webster.) People who are good at manipulating emotions are usually artful at making others experience guilt or shame, as well as causing them to experience joy and hope. Manipulation is a form of witchcraft when it relies on evil sources for power or is fueled by self-centered motives.

> "Witchcraft is the manipulation or controlling spirit, regardless of who it comes through...The mother who manipulates her son or daughter into marrying her choice has done it through witchcraft, and such relationships usually have to be held together through manipulation and control. The prayer group that uses prayers to expose others is gossiping for the sake of manipulation; this is not prayer—it is witchcraft... Spiritual leaders who use manipulation, hype or control to build their church or ministry are operating in a counterfeit spiritual authority equivalent to witchcraft." (*Overcoming Witchcraft,* Joyner, 2010)

Charismatic Witchcraft is using the magical seduction of a personality to handle or control others, especially the emotions of others, for unrighteous purposes. Satan, the enemy of God and the enemy of our souls, is a manipulator. He is a liar and a deceiver. He uses manipulation as one of his tools in his arsenal. His schemes include preying on the weak and the hurt, (like a roaring lion searching for prey); fostering insecurity and despair; creating fear and confusion; causing discord among the body; and inciting pride among God's people. He knows that pride goes before the fall.

Good manipulators have mastered the enemy's tactics, and may add a few of their own such as vilifying and/or blaming the victim; withholding information or lying by omission; using God as a cloak for their own desires and motives. For example, they lead in with a statement such as: "The Holy Spirit says to the church…" And, they end with something conjured up in a planning session to raise more money. When you hear, "thus sayeth the Lord", be sure it is a genuine gift of prophecy, not the manipulative skills of a charismatic leader. In the church setting, the person with the microphone has the audience's attention and therefore has the best chance of manipulation. The degree of skill, charisma, and persuasion displayed is proportionate to the level of excitement generated and the level of degree of credibility ascribed to the message—whatever it is. Such is the advantage of the pusher in the pulpit.

The street pusher may also have the gift of gab, a charming personality, and ability to persuade—though very little sales-manship is needed once an addict is hooked. "This drug will make you reach a high that no one has ever reached before. Man! It will be so good, that before you finish inhaling the first hit, you will be thinking about how to raise money for some more." Or, as Ms. M has told us, "This drug is designed especially for you, because you are my best and special customer."

Crack cocaine continues to be one of the most popular street drugs, even today. Why? Because charismatic drug dealers know how to push it, and they profit greatly from it. Sadly enough, because of the sudden rush of euphoria, most users don't realize the manipulation behind the availability of the drug. The pusher's primary goal is to control, to dominate and to manipulate his clients into a relationship of dependency, then codependency, which causes the pusher to gain authority over their lives. The more addicts, the more money he makes. It's just that simple. If only innocent people would understand the scheme behind the euphoria!

Ms. M slowly learned how to gain the favor of her pusher. She was "reliable." He could call on her any time night or day and she could persuade people to buy from him. In exchange for making big sales, Ms. M got to smoke as much as she wanted. Ms. M was middle-management. Sure, it meant that sometimes she took the hit for the team and landed in jail. She learned to adjust to jail. And when she felt down, with a moment of sanity and remorse, her pusher would say, "you'll be alright—here, smoke this with me." He would fill her head with compliments of how valuable she was to him, and use flattery and encouragement to manipulate her emotions and to keep her connected to him. She operated also with a spirit of charisma as she persuaded others to buy from her pusher. No wonder he wanted to keep her around.

Well, life for the unsuspecting addict is no different in the Church at large. Many church leaders around the world can be equated with pushers. The resemblance lies in the intentional manipulation and control of innocent people often for the pure sake of the profit they yield. Again, if only the innocent would understand the scheme behind the euphoria!

> *"Be self-controlled and alert. Your enemy the devil prowls around like a roaring lion looking for someone to devour. Resist him, standing firm in the faith because you know that your brothers throughout the world are undergoing the same kind of sufferings. And the God of all grace, who called you to His eternal glory in Christ, after you have suffered a little while, will Himself restore you and make you strong, firm and steadfast."* (1 Peter 5: 8—10, NIV)

Lions attack sick, young and straggling animals. The weaker they are, the greater the victim. Their influence is tremendous. They leave lasting imprints on their victims, if they don't kill them. Their attack is intentional. It is damning to the victims. Lions are ferocious, frightening, and forceful. They have but one goal in mind, to overtake and control the lives of their victims. As ferocious as the devil is and even when he seems to have us in the grip of his attack, Peter admonishes us never to forget that our God will rescue and restore us. He will restore our health, our finances, our families, our faith and our futures, but we must also be aware of Satan's modis operandi in order to avoid the attacks.

In his article, "Overcoming Witchcraft", Rick Joyner (2010) helps us understand how to both recognize and overcome this insidious practice:

> "Understanding Satan's schemes significantly increases our advantage in the battle. The entire church age has been one of spiritual warfare and it is increasing as we approach the end of it. Satan is now being cast out of the heavenlies and down to the earth where he is coming with great wrath, but we need not fear—He who is in us is *much greater* than he who is in the world. He who is least in the kingdom of God has more power than any antichrist. But just as the greatest military power today is vulnerable if it does not recognize the enemy's attack, we too are vulnerable if we do not recognize Satan's schemes. The only way that he can defeat us is by our own ignorance or complacency. As we maintain our position in Christ, take on the full armor of God and remain vigilant, we will not only stand but prevail against the gates of hell." (Joyner, 2010)

Witchcraft, including charismatic witchcraft, uses counterfeit spiritual authority; it is using an unholy spirit to dominate, manipulate or control others. The apostle Paul named witchcraft (also called "sorcery" as discussed in chapter 1) as one of the works of the flesh (Galatians 5:20). The basic defense against counterfeit spiritual authority is to walk in true spiritual authority. Establishing our lives on truth and trust in the Lord to accomplish what concerns us is essential if we are going to be free of the influence and pressure of witchcraft (Joyner, 2010).

Saul and David are examples of biblical characters with two types of spiritual authority. While Saul relied heavily on his personal charisma, and later on witchcraft to rule the people, David relied on the Lord.

> "King Saul is a personification of one who was ordained by God but fell from his place of true spiritual authority to operate in counterfeit spiritual authority. King David is a personification of true spiritual authority. How did David react to Saul? He was willing to serve the house of Saul until Saul chased him away. Even then he never retaliated, rebelled or tried to undermine Saul's authority, but honored him as "the Lord's anointed". Even though David was called to take Saul's place, he never lifted his hand against Saul, but determined that if God had really called him, then He would have to establish him—he demonstrated the exact opposite of the manipulative or controlling spirit and by that overcame the evil with good. Had David manipulated his way into the kingdom, he would have almost certainly fallen to witchcraft just like Saul. But David was of a different spirit." (Joyner, 2010)

David countered Saul's episodic demonic evil spirit with an attitude of respect for his authority and service. Saul, on the other hand, manipulated his own son, Jonathan, to gain access to David's whereabouts in order to do him harm. "Hey son, let me know when David, your best friend comes, so I can kill him..." He quickly changed from an attitude of appreciation for David's services to an attitude of vengeful aggression. "David, my boy, play me a nice song and soothe my headache, and while you are there let me use you for target practice for my javelin, because I am secretly jealous of you!" Oh, the wicked machinations of counterfeit spiritual authority.

One of the critical characteristics of those with authentic spiritual authority is that they seek the Lord before, during, and after making decisions. One of the most frequent phrases attributed to David was "*he inquired of the Lord*". On the other hand, Saul was known to seek the consultation of a witch when he was uncertain and fearful of how or if he could defeat the enemy.

> "The manipulation and control spirits gains entrance through FEAR. It is the fearful and insecure who become so obsessed with controlling others that they use evil influence, and it will take a demonstration of perfect love to cast out these fears." (Joyner, 2010)

When Satan comes against the church, he attacks the leader as well as the body. Like Saul, even the anointed can fall prey to satanic attacks. Depression, fear, despair, confusion, defeat are but some of the negative emotions the enemy uses to gain access to our spirits. The presence of these deadly emotions should be signs that the enemy has a foothold. If these emotions are generated from the pulpit, then the likelihood that there is a pusher in the pulpit is great.

Let me say here—that those of us who are called, appointed and anointed are influential. And, we are supposed to be influential, but our influence ought to line up with the Word of God and should never leave the persons we minister to even more confused or depressed. When we are influenced to think, feel, and behave in ways that are not consistent with the Word of

God, we have been as addicts in the pews. We have replaced our standard for living, no longer using the Bible as our standard, but the unspoken rules of the church (and I'll get to this in a later chapter) as delivered by a charismatic preacher have now become our standard for living. This is not right, and we are lured into this because of charismatic pastors and charismatic church leaders. Charisma is necessary and needed, but to be charismatic to the point of attaching people to oneself falsely or making it seem like an authentic attachment, is abusing the gift. This is abuse as opposed to reaching out to people.

The Bible declares that Jesus called the twelve to Him (to Him is indicative of relationship), thus, they were close to Him and He was able to mentor them, pour into them, teach them and correct them, lead and guide them into all truth. He did that intentionally. They were with Him in his down sittings and His uprising. They were with Him at various sundry times during His ministry. Where others were not permitted, they were permitted to be with Him. So, ministry is relational—Jesus was not only charismatic, He was relational.

According to Peter Scazzero (2003), as he speaks about the emotionally-healthy church, one of the things that wreck church and relationships is that many church leaders do not understand real, right, and healthy relationships. They, therefore, lure unsuspecting, weak, emotionally broken individuals into their traps—people who feel like if they can get connected to this type of charisma, then everything in their lives will be alright. The emotionally-needy person has a misconception of how to attain more perceived power, and now they are not looking to the Holy Spirit to be empowered, but looking to the charismatic leader to tie them to his arm and lead them on. Now there's an emotional attachment that is not only unhealthy, but unholy and not what thus sayeth God! It has nothing to do with the sanctification process; nothing to do with growing in God; nothing to do with growing up as a leader in God; nothing to do with being developed and matured in God, as Paul says, it has nothing to do with equipping the saints—it serves, not the people, but it serves his or her own demented disease and that is his own quest for power and control.

You may ask, how does one become emotionally manipulated by the charismatic leader? It happens when charismatic leaders or church leaders have no intention of being relational with the people they lead, but because one has a gift, they are "special". So, they prostitute your gifts. Herein lies the problem, in the 20/80 rule (and most churches run off a 20/80 rule—20% of the people doing the work and 80% are spectators) it is believed that in the 80% there are no gifts. The devil is a liar and the father of lies (John 8:44)!! There are myriad gifts in that 80%, but when you have a gift recognized by unhealed and unchecked emotionally-unhealthy leaders, there is something special about that recognition. First, you feel singled out and special, and if the charismatic leader is abusing his or her own gifts, you can be sure that yours will be abused also. The anointing can be seductive. The problem in the church today is that so many people use their anointing as seduction. And, when they reach out to you, your selfish need for recognition allows you to ignore all red flags, because suddenly, you have a platform to also place your gifts on display. So, you join the ranks of the sick and broken gifted who are made to feel special, by someone equally sick and broken.

Let me use my own story—I said that I was broken when I came to the church. Because I learned the art of charisma (and yes indeed there are some gifts that God has endowed me with), I was able to use charisma to cover up my own sickness. I was able to use my own charismatic design to overwhelm people so much, that nobody ever saw what was going on underneath. I was broken, I was boarder-line alcoholic and the church didn't care. All they were concerned about was my charisma—was I on my post doing my thing? Was I drawing in people who would later be giving major offerings? I was drawing in people, but nobody was ever concerned about my healing. It was charismatic witchcraft—but I was special, and I felt at the time in my own demented mind that I was really connected.

Protecting yourself from charismatic witchcraft and emotional manipulation

Everyone who calls him or herself a Christian is vulnerable to satanic attacks. Because the enemy is relentless in his pursuit of kingdom builders, if you are reading this, chances are that he has been on your trail, too. Of course this is easy to admit—people of God are the main target for the enemy. More difficult to admit is the fact that men and women of God also are sometimes the very persons practicing under demonic influence. Before we gear up to ward off external attacks from the enemy, we must first confront the enemy within. Deliverance means we must first repent of the ways we have allowed ourselves to be used by the enemy.

"Therefore, the first principle in being delivered from the influence of witchcraft is to repent of all the ways that we ourselves have used it and to keep it out of our own life and ministry. What God is building is not raised up by might or power, but by His Spirit. Whatever we build by other means is an affront to the cross and will ultimately oppose that which the Spirit is doing. The flesh wars against the Spirit, regardless of how good we try to make the flesh look." (Joyner, 2010)

After we have repented of our own sins follow these guidelines to protect yourself from charismatic witchcraft.

1. Do not return evil for evil (Romans 12:17); instead, bless those who curse you (Romans 12:14).

The Word of the Lord says, we must not return evil for evil but overcome evil with good (Romans 12:21). A blessing is more powerful and carries more weight than a curse. Why? Because a true blessing taps into the heart of God and joins His will for that person. The Word of God says that the fruit of the spirit is love, joy, peace, patience, kindness, goodness, faithfulness, gentleness and self-control. (Galatians 5:22-23)

"We are defeated by the enemy when he can get us to respond in any spirit other than the Holy Spirit, whose fruit is love, joy, peace, etc. The enemy's strategy is to get us to depart from the Holy Spirit and living by the fruit of the Spirit to try to combat him on his own terms...That is why the basic strategy we must use to begin freeing ourselves from the power of witchcraft is to bless those who curse us. This does not mean bless their works, but that we pray for them and not against them. We are not warring against flesh and blood and the weapons of our warfare are not carnal, but spiritual. When we begin to pray blessing upon the people who are attacking us, then the evil power of control and manipulation is broken over them and us." (Joyner, 2010)

2. Ask for the gift of discernment and know the true power of God

The Word of God says, "God is Spirit and those who worship Him must worship Him in spirit and truth". (John 4:24) In order to receive the true power of God, we must experience God in a truly spiritual way. We must be careful not to be caught up in the form or fashion of the worship experience. We must not be hypocritical in the way we serve Him. Our worship must be a true reflection of our love for Him. Our lives must also reflect the same. As we extend ourselves to Him, and lose ourselves in Him, it is only then that we can experience the true power of God.

> "The first defense against the deceptive supernatural power of the enemy is to know the true power of God...
> "As we walk in faith, that which we begin to see with the eyes of our heart starts to become more real to us than what we are seeing with our natural eyes. We take a major step in being delivered from the power of witchcraft when we start to see the Lord so clearly that we serve and respect Him more than anything else; then we are no longer subject to the influence, manipulation

and control of those who are still earthly minded, or who move in the power of witchcraft."(Joyner, 2010)

I found a delightful article on the website of Glorious Praise Worship Center about spiritual discernment. The gift of discernment of spirits is a primary gift of the Holy Spirit enabling us to exercise Godly wisdom in less than apparent matters. It is especially used in the context of discerning spirits, whether they are good or evil. Discernment is not a result of a gut feeling of suspiciousness or feeling negative emotions. It is the result of being filled with the Holy Spirit and of manifesting the fruits of the Spirit.

> "True spiritual discernment is rooted in love that *"is kind, patient, not jealous, does not brag, is not arrogant, does not act unbecomingly, does not seek its own, is not provoked, does not take into account a wrong suffered, does not rejoice in unrighteousness, but rejoices in the truth; bears all things, believes all things, hopes all things, endures all things"* (1 Corinthians 13:4-7).* Unless we are seeing through the eyes of God's love, we are not seeing clearly and we will not interpret accurately what we see. True discernment can only operate through God's love...God's love is utterly pure and easily distinguishes between the pure and the impure, but it always does it for the right reasons." (Glorious Praise, 2009)

"Insecurity, self-preservation, self-promotion, unhealed wounds, unforgiveness, bitterness, etc. will all confuse and neutralize true spiritual discernment" (Glorious Praise, 2009). In fact, many people who appear spiritual, who are not yet healed from emotional wounds, will acknowledge difficulty with discernment. It is little wonder that they fall prey to the same forms of victimization again and again. I also found it interesting that as I began to walk in true spiritual authority, there were persons who would avoid close contact with me, as if I would expose their counterfeit authority. They knew that I could not be negatively influenced or manipulated, so instead of drawing nearer to me, they literally moved quickly in the other direction when they saw me coming.

3. Prepare for warfare by putting on the armor of God

Christians have but one option. We must do spiritual warfare if we want to survive. All Christians must prepare themselves to battle the enemy. A properly trained soldier would not think of going into battle without the appropriate gear. Using a battle-readiness analogy of the time, Ephesians 6:10-18 describes the full armor of God.

> [11]*Put on the full armor of God so that you can take your stand against the devil's schemes.* [12]*For our struggle is not against flesh and blood, but against the rulers, against the authorities, against the powers of this dark world and against the spiritual forces of evil in the heavenly realms.* [13]*Therefore put on the full armor of God, so that when the day of evil comes, you may be able to stand your ground, and after you have done everything, to stand.* [14]*Stand firm then, with the belt of truth buckled around your waist, with the breastplate of righteousness in place,* [15]*and with your feet fitted with the readiness that comes from the gospel of peace.* [16]*In addition to all this, take up the shield of faith, with which you can extinguish all the flaming arrows of the evil one.* [17]*Take the helmet of salvation and the sword of the Spirit, which is the word of God.* [18]*And pray in the*

Spirit on all occasions with all kinds of prayers and requests. With this in mind, be alert and always keep on praying for all the saints.

Protect your most vulnerable parts with truth, protect your heart with righteousness, stand on peace, hold out your faith which is the first line of defense, fight back with the word, your only offensive weapon and keep praying. This is how Christians fight witchcraft, sorcery, or any diabolical attack from the enemy.

"All of these are required for every spiritual victory. Anything less will result in less than a victory; we may make occasional, halting advances, but we will sooner or later be pushed back. But it is clear at the end of the age there will be an army of God raised up that will not settle for occasional advances—They have committed themselves to the fight and will not stop until there is the complete victory over the enemy that is promised. It is understood that the total victory will not be accomplished without the personal return of the Lord, but we must fight until He comes, and fight to take every bit of ground that we can, until His appearing when He takes us up to return with Him and finish the fight. 'The earth is the Lord's and all it contains'" (Psalm 24:1). Until the earth has been completely recovered from the domain of Satan our fight is not over.'" (Glorious Praise, 2009)

This is the posture of the church I pastor. I am determined that the church is an army. In this season where the enemy is waging all out warfare against the things of God, it is my intent, (in my small corner of the earth), to no longer raise members, but true missionaries. To no longer raise loiterers but Christian leaders. To no longer nurture victims but raise victors. To no longer raise just winners but warriors. Let's not get it twisted, the church is in a fight!; a fight for the correct representation of our Christ; a fight for the correct representation of His church; a fight for the correct representation of His life. We need men and women of God who will not only learn His word but will dare to live His word. We need leaders who will publicly pronounce their wrongs and will eagerly seek peace and pursue it. We need people who were once lost but know of the healing power of Almighty God to profess to those who have never experienced Him, that YES, God is real! Beloved, we are in a fight!!!

His church receives the brunt of society's reflections as to who Christians are and who they are not. The church serves as Christ's representation on the earth and as such, we should always be reflective and responsible for any and all actions that do not represent the Christ we say we love. We must fight to get the CHURCH back!!!

4. Resist the enemy and cause him to flee.

> *Submit yourselves, then, to God. Resist the devil, and he will flee from you.* (James 4:7)

The sequence of the above scripture is important. First we must submit ourselves to God, then we must resist the devil. Submitting to God means to turn your will over to Him, which will then lead to obedience. Resisting the devil means that we put up a good fight to protect the things that he is most interest in destroying. The devil comes to make us doubt God, and he comes to steal God's words from our hearts. Resisting the devil means standing strongly on your faith, and speaking boldly, the Word of the Lord. When you do this, the devil is intimidated by your strength, and he goes out looking for weaker prey!

5. Gain control over your own emotions by using the Word of God

*For God hath not given us the spirit of fear; but of power, and of love, and of a **sound mind**.* 2 Timothy 1:7 (KJV)

*For God is not the **author** of **confusion**, but of peace, as in all churches of the saints.* Corinthians 14:33 (KJV)

Fear, depression, discouragement, defeat, confusion, does not come from God. He is the author of faith and the hope which never disappoints. One writer says that when one experiences these emotions they are having a crisis of faith. "FAITH is the fruit of the Spirit and the shield of our armor that counters discouragement. If we begin to get discouraged it is because we have dropped our shield. Pick it back up!"

Self-focus breeds depression. Focus on the goodness of God, do what's right, continue in the spiritual disciplines of prayer, fasting, reading the word daily, and forgiving self and others. A friend of mine used an acrostic that I love to ensure emotional health: SIMPLIFY (Jenkins-Hall, 2004). SIMPLIFY is an acrostic for eight spiritual disciplines that will help with your emotional health. Practice the disciplines of solitude, introspection, meditation, prayer, letting go (forgiving others and self), intentional sacrifice, fasting and yielding. Regulate your emotions by staying in the will of God. This will increase your ability to resist emotional manipulation when it comes your way.

6. Stay humble before the Lord

> *"Humble yourselves, therefore, under the mighty hand of God, that He may exalt you at the proper time."* (1 Peter 5:6)"

There is nothing that will more quickly destroy our ability to walk in true spiritual authority than self-seeking, self-promotion or self-preservation. (Joyner, 2010) *"God opposes the proud, but gives grace to the humble" (James 4:6).* Therefore, if we have wisdom we will seek humility before position. True authority operates on the grace of God, and the more authority we walk in, the more grace we need. We only have true spiritual authority to the degree that the King lives within us. True spiritual authority is not a position; it is grace. Counterfeit spiritual authority stands on its position instead of grace. The highest spiritual authority, Jesus, used His position to lay down His life. He commanded those who would come after Him to take up their crosses to do the same.

> "Any authority or influence that we gain by our own manipulation or self-promotion will be a stumbling block to us and our ability to receive a true commission and authority from God. If we are going to walk in true spiritual authority, like David, we will have to utterly trust in the Lord to establish us in it and in His time." (Joyner, 2010)

The Word of the Lord says in 2 Corinthians 2:14 that there is no failure in Christ. Because we are in Him, if we rely on Him, we will always win. Not only do we win, but we wear the perfume of victory in Christ, and we spread the fragrance to others, encouraging them to also claim their victories.

> *But thanks be to God, who always leads us in triumphal procession in Christ and through us spreads everywhere the fragrance of the knowledge of him.* (2 Corinthians 2:14, NIV)

Defeat is not an option in Christ. The one and only way we can be defeated is to not be in Him. Romans 8:37 reminds us that we are more than conquerors through Him who loves us. It is God's plan to redeem His church. The ultimate redemption will be ours after Jesus Christ returns, but while we wait, we have been endued with spiritual power that comes from the Holy Spirit dwelling in us. We have power enough to overcome any witchcraft, be it geared towards manipulation of our hearts, our emotions, or our intellect. The next chapter considers a different but related kind of witchcraft—the use of words and misuse of God's Word to dominate our intellect.

Personal Reflections:

The idea of blindly usurping the desire for the will of God out of the lives of His people and skillfully replacing it with one's own, is masterful deception and trickery. At the heart of the shepherd should always be the development and growth of the flock. Our role as leaders is to deliberately point lives towards Christ, towards His will, towards His goals for our living. I remember a question raised in a Bible Study session one night. The question was, "What is it that keeps people from obeying the will of God for their lives?" Many responded;

finances, careers, inadequacies and the like. I remember raising my hand and saying, "While all that may be true, and may play a small role in the equation, I believe the greatest deterrent from following and obeying the will of God is this: When you place your life in the hands of God, you remove it from the hands of man." At that point, manipulation no longer works! At that point, intimidation no longer works! At that point, domination no longer wins! Emotions are managed, fears are overcome, ambitions are guided, and destiny is eminent. Isn't this the place a pastor *wants* for his/her parishioners? Reflect on these questions.

1. Do people easily control what you think or how you feel?

2. What scriptures have you memorized to ward off the attacks of the enemy?

3. Which if any of these areas of vulnerability leave you open for the attack of the enemy?
    a. Insecurity
    b. Unwillingness to trust others/overconfidence in yourself
    c. Unhealed emotions from the past
    d. Passivity/lack of assertiveness in doing what you know is right

4. Do you have a discerning spirit? How do you know?

CHAPTER SEVEN

HERMENEUTIC MANIPULATION
(INTELLECTUALLY DOMINATED)

"For the time will come when men will not put up with sound doctrine. Instead, to suit their own desires, they will gather around them a great number of teachers to say what their itching ears want to hear." (2 Timothy 4:3, NIV)

Many teachers, preachers and pastors talk about the pursuit of knowledge, but often they don't want knowledge, they want power. These people won't listen to sound doctrine, instead they turn their ears away to myths. You can see this everywhere—from liberal churches to college campuses, people claiming to have a bit more enlightenment than what the Bible has to say; people claiming to improve upon God's words. According to the life application commentary of the NIV, these people have several things in common:

1. They do not tolerate the truth. They have no interest or respect for absolute truth or any standard for judgment. They create their own standards.

2. They reject truth for sensationalism. They want truth that only fits their situation and works for them at that

time. What they feel, what works for them, what seems compelling—that is their truth and they claim absolute right to it. No one should even attempt to tell them differently.

3. They gather viewpoints to suit their selfish desires. Although they profess objectivity, their only defense for their viewpoints is a: its mine; and b: it suits my desires.

Such teachers have a following because they are telling the people what their itching ears want to hear. These people are following myths. Like Timothy, you must "keep your head in all situations" and seek God's Word for the truth (Life Application Bible; NIV; pg. 2051).

Let me explain each of these points:

1. They do not tolerate truth—In these cases, leaders have determined that they live "above" the truth. Truth here means God's Word. They are not held accountable for truth. This is indicative of the problem that lies with independent churches and leaders. There is no accountability. Therefore, church leaders easily become rulers of their own worlds with the need for personal accountability to no one. I am reminded of a situation that called for Christian leadership. It involved the utter shattering of another brother's character and integrity. A third-party leader pointed out the scripture that teaches how we should handle such a situation. He was told by the leader, "I don't have to do that". (*That* referred to what the Bible says.) These unchecked

leaders force the Bible on unsuspecting and innocent lives when they themselves have no regard for the truth.

2. They also have no regard for a second kind of truth: that which is real and true. To speak absolute truth to these leaders is not acceptable and if done is often used as grounds for dismissal. These leaders are experts, therefore in creating cultures of silence in which no one is allowed to speak truth to power. People are silently taught to live in the fear of ever breathing real "truth".

3. They reject truth for sensationalism—If it fits my needs I will accept it. If it works to my advantage, I will accept it. If I can twist it without these idiots recognizing it, I can use it. What a travesty!!!!

They gather viewpoints to suit their own selfish desires—whatever will help defend their case, is the viewpoint they will receive! For many of these leaders, there are only a few voices they will even listen to, often from people who carry their same spirit. These other kindred voices usually serve deceptively and with false loyalty for the life of the ministry. They each are not able to even recognize the detriment they are to each other because they carry the same spirit and serve the same demented disease: A quest for power and control. Alas, many lives have suffered at the hands of this twisted combination.

Psalm 119, the longest Psalm, is replete with references to the importance of the law, which is the Word of God. The psalmist takes pleasure in the Word. It is his guiding light, his hope and his salvation. His obedience to the Word ensures his good success. Without the Word physically in his hand, it must be written on his heart. For only then can he be assured immediate access to his sword and his shield. So, the psalmist meditates on the Word day and night. *"Thy Word have I hid in my heart, that I might not sin against Thee" (Psa. 119:11).*

In the previous verse, David asks for help. He asks to be preserved from wandering. In verse 11, he takes deliberate precaution to keep himself from falling into sin. Thy Word have I hid in mine heart. His heart would be kept by the Word because he kept the word in his heart. All that David knew of the written word, and all that had been revealed to him by the voice of God; he had stored away *all,* without exception, in his affections, as a treasure to be preserved in a coffer. The Word in his heart could also been compared to a choice seed to be buried in a fruitful soil, and, what soil is more fruitful than a renewed heart, wholly seeking the Lord?

The Word was God's own, and therefore precious to God's servant. He did not wear a text on his heart as a charm, but he hid it in his heart as a rule. He laid it up knowing that it would keep him, and it would save him from himself. We must imitate David, copying his heart work as well as his outward character. First, we must mind that what we believe is truly God's word; that being done, we must hide or treasure it —each person for him or herself. We must see that this is done, not as a mere feat of the memory, but as the joyful act of the affections. It should be a joy to call from the heart, the saving, sustaining and correcting word of the Lord!

That I might not sin against thee. Here was the object aimed at. As someone has well said: Here is the best thing,"thy word";

hidden in the best place, "in my heart;" for the best of purposes, "that I might not sin against thee." This was done by David with personal care, as a man carefully hides away his money when he fears thieves. In this case, the thief he dreaded was sin. God's Word is the best prevention against offending God, for it tells us his mind and will, and tends to bring our spirit into conformity with the divine Spirit. No cure for sin in the life is equal to the word in the seat of life, which is the heart. There is no hiding from sin unless we hide the Word. If we are not going to cause God displeasure, His Word MUST be our treasure.

Unlike the psalmist, the average Christian rarely reads the Word of God and certainly does not meditate on the Word day and night. The days of memorizing and reciting scriptures in church are but faded memories. In fact, one of the greatest travesties in the church today is negligence in studying the Word of God, resulting in ignorance of the Word.

When parishioners do not study and gain understanding of the Word of God for themselves they subject themselves to false interpretation and manipulation of God's Word. They also deprive themselves of the promises of God intended for their lives. When church leaders are permitted to use scripture to support manipulative tactics, this practice is known as "Hermeneutic Manipulation", and often goes unnoticed and therefore unchecked. Hermeneutics is the science of biblical interpretation, afforded anyone with proper study and application of interpretive principles. This is not limited to a pastor, teacher or apostle but is available to all. When a person does not read the Bible or explore its interpretation, they open themselves to intellectual domination.

A crack addict has heard the words of warning and correction time and time again. For young children, teachers, parents and the church alike provide instructions that if heeded are designed to keep us from falling. Truth is certain to guard us from evil and to secure our understanding of that which is false. To obey the words of parents, Sunday school teachers and classroom teachers, may serve as preventative to that child, saving the child from many of life's sordid difficulties. Simply remembering what "mama n'em" said is often a pivotal moment of making a decision for our well-being or to our self-destruction. It is as if we have a tape recorder hidden in our minds or hearts that replays those priceless words of wisdom at precisely the right moments in our lives. Don't take candy from strangers. Don't do drugs. Stay away from strangers. Say please and thank you...each of us has a list of the words from our parents that we have hidden in our hearts as treasured guidelines for life, even after our parents have passed on.

There is no question that words are important to our lives. The power of life and death both reside in the tongue (Proverbs 18:21). The tongue seems like a small, insignificant part of our bodies, but it controls and influences much (James 3:5).

The Apostle Paul warns Timothy to: **Study** to shew thyself approved unto God, a workman that needeth not to be ashamed, rightly dividing the word of truth (2 Timothy 2:15). Like Timothy, we are also encouraged to study to equip ourselves to handle God's Word rightly. Today, one only has to surf the Internet to find hundreds of websites with complete, sound expository commentaries on most major passages of scripture in the Bible. Or, simply reading the text in the many different versions of the Bible at our fingertips, with the guidance of the Holy Spirit, helps us discern the true and proper meaning of scripture. However, rather than studying the Word for ourselves, we are lulled into complacency, easily manipulated by a pusher in the pulpit.

Similar to how a drug pusher cuts his best cocaine powder with flour in order to be more profitable, the manipulative pusher in the pulpit also dilutes the Word of God for his or her own profit or advantage. Rather than preaching the Word with hermeneutic simplicity and purity, he or she laces it with human wisdom, a well-placed metaphor, or a hodgepodge of razzle-dazzle alliterations to tickle the listener's untrained ear.

I earlier stated that the impetus for this book was a study of Acts 16:16, where there appeared a damsel operating in "the things of God," yet possessed by a spirit of divination. This damsel spoke boldly as a prophet might, yet without Godly authority or intent. It is possible to speak the Word of God in the absence of the Spirit of God. Hermeneutics is a science that teaches the skill that produces the ability to rightly divide. When you are an addict in the pews and you have charismatic leadership, you have already been lured and you are so "in it" and everything they say, you take as truth—without questioning, without reading for yourself. That is Hermeneutic Manipulation!!

Were you ever made to feel stupid by your pusher? This question I asked of my friend, Ms. M. Her response was, "Yes!

He never called me stupid, but he always spoke for me." What is it about churches where leadership does not want to hear the voice of their congregants? I'm a pastor, and we are only pastors because we have people, so where this disconnect comes from I just don't understand. Now, pastoring does not place us in heights of supremacy. It is a gift that God has endowed us with and is a calling upon our lives to lead and guide the people of God into all truth. It is not to dictate to them, or legislate their behavior. It is to lead them in truth, so they can live their best lives.

Now clarity is necessary here—there is one primary voice in leadership. Where there is a pastor, that should be the only decisive voice that we hear. He is charged with soul care and is the ultimate voice the congregants expect to hear, especially regarding matters of vision and direction for the church. That is not the context I'm talking about. The context I'm talking about is when a question is thrown out in a leadership meeting such as, "What are some reasons we are losing momentum in our young adult population? "–and nobody wants to give a truthful answer. Instead people take the opportunity to say what a wonderful job the pastor is doing teaching and preaching. The problem is that the answers tickle the leader's ears and are far from the truth. If a brave soldier dares to speak a bit of reality, his comments are turned against him, in favor of what the leader believes is the real issue. The truth is often disclosed only after the meeting in the parking lot or on the way home over cell phones: sermons are too long, the offering appeals are too frequent, the ministry demands are not family-oriented, young adults are not respected, their ideas are often second-guessed, and accused of not being spiritual enough. So, cultures of silence are created where people are not allowed to speak truthfully and when they do, they are made to regret it later. Thus, the leader is clueless about the heart of the people in the pews of his or her own ministry.

Here's the real reality in many environments like the one that I'm describing—the real reality is these are not stupid people. So, behind closed doors there are countless conversations with people who have great understanding of the Word of God and have great spirits of discernment and know that what they are discerning is dead wrong. Because of the culture, I am now not only engulfed by the charisma, I'm engulfed by the hermeneutic. I'll take the Word of the Lord and not even look at it for myself, trusting that everything my charismatic leader is saying to me must be right. Why? Because now he's my idol!! Now my worship has shifted. It's hero worship and it's no longer the worship of our true and living God. Now we're involved in personality worship. If I allow my own truth to come out, then I know that this personality "will go slam off" on me!

The Apostle Paul spoke much about this. He said, "Beware of false prophets who come as ravenous wolves, but are dressed in sheep's clothing." Paul warned us that this day would come—when people would be afraid to speak truth. One of the travesties in the body of Christ—not in a particular church, but in the body of Christ—is this whole piece about speaking truth to power. Most leaders have a perceived power—they have little real power. That's why many in the churches are not healed. If those leaders were walking in any kind of real authority and anointing, those demons would not be sitting in front rows. Demons would not be allowed to teach. Demons would not be allowed to stay in the house without being cleansed. The Bible says the Holy Spirit comes to convict us of sin and we are not to condone it, but to expose it. But when you have no power to expose, then we have wrong operating in what looks like right. You have hurt and emotionally-broken people, like myself, coming and attaching themselves to fellowships and congregations who are not postured for their healing. This occurs every day, and in every city in America, and even around the world. By and large, every race, every creed, every culture, and every indigenous group is potentially affected by unhealthy church practices. Sadly, in most churches around the world, there is church manipulation, there is charismatic witchcraft, there is hermeneutic manipulation and there is legalistic control. Why? Because where people are vulnerable and broken, there is opportunity for control and manipulation. The vulnerable lose their voices and partake of prophetic crack. Beware, beloved. There are addicts in the pews and pushers in the pulpit!!

One of the questions in the interview with Ms. M, our former drug addict was, "Why would you stay with a certain pusher, when you could get your drugs from any place"? Her response was, "Every time I tried to go to another pusher, he'd give me a job to do, and so it made me feel like I was connected to him."

The parallel of that in the church with addicts in the pews, is when people try to break free, they are often made to believe that the leader can't do without them. They are told, "I've got an assignment, and God has identified you to carry it out". They make you feel so special and as if nobody can do this but you. So addicts stay around to support the pusher because they are "needed" and they are "special". I asked my friend, Ms. M, "How did you help him?" Her response was, "I told others how good his product was. So, other people trusted me—if it was good enough for Ms. M, it was good enough for them."

My life was no different in the church. In fact, now as a pastor, I've come to realize that several people were in the same church with me only because I was there. If it's good enough for me, it's good enough for them.

> "Satan has ministers who preach from the Word of God in the pulpits every Sunday. They sound really good to the unsuspecting. They have and share many doctrinal truths that are found in Scripture, but there is always a catch. They are subtly preaching another Jesus and another gospel. The Word warns us concerning this: 2 Peter 2:1 *But there were false prophets also among the people, even as there shall be false teachers among you, who privily shall bring in damnable heresies, even denying the Lord that bought them, and bring upon themselves swift destruction.*" (Oliver Greene, Acts of the Apostles Commentary, vol. 3)

Interesting to note of these false prophets is this; they don't even realize the destruction they are bringing upon themselves. From my personal experience, many others to include myself have been blamed for "their personal destruction". The desperate need for a "scapegoat" in the lives of these heretics is incredible. A scapegoat is one who takes the indirect hit for the failures of others. These false leaders must have someone else to blame for their own private destruction. Sadly enough, they will use their pulpits often to discredit others.

In fact, I can recall countless stories of leaders who were in such modes of destruction that they sought to defame anyone who would not stand in agreement with them. The need for the raping of one's character is extremely important for these leaders. They must remove attention from themselves for, remember, truth is only truth when it works to their advantage! I have seen innocent lives discredited at the hands of faulty leadership. Although those discredited have gone on to do great works for God, my heart aches for the many who receive these lies as truth and then turn on innocent people. We must be aware of wolves dressed in sheep's clothing!

The average minister spends several hours a week thinking about the message God would have him or her deliver to the people. Many things are considered when praying over the message: the needs of the body, the vision of the ministry, the movement of God in the life of the preacher or the persons closest to him or her. The preacher starts by seeking a ministering and inspiring word. Then Satan enters in and brings to mind the situations of the week that gave rise to anger, frustration, and irritation. Slowly, the messenger begins to "hear from God" through scripture just what he needs to say to avenge himself or to direct the body to a certain response to that frustrating situation. For example, someone borrowed a large sum of money from the church and soon after left the church. A message about Jesus coming in the rapture like a thief in the night may take a conspicuous turn to warn, "beware of thieves in the night!"

The work of the enemy is subtle. We must be careful to always pray that God hides us behind his sacred cross, so that our own fleshly impulses and motives are not interjected.

> "There are so-called "Christians" who come to church every Sunday. Some are demon-possessed. Some are preachers and teachers. They claim to hear from God. They sit as tares among the wheat. They gossip and they sow discord among brethren, and all the while appear so spiritual. The devil does not sit in your church with horns and a pitchfork." (Oliver Greene, Acts of the Apostles Commentary, vol. 3)

The devil is cunning and clever and therefore dresses to please the environment, looks to please the environment and ultimately fits right into the environment. Unless you have a keen sense of discernment, you would never know how evil some of these imposters are! An unsuspecting pew addict would never look to a Sunday school teacher as anything other than a role model, sent from God. How surprising it is to find that he or she is also a big gossiper, a major liar, or always stirring up mischief. How can you tell when that same person prays "better" than any one you've ever heard, or leads the ministry into praise and worship in a way that seems to be directing the congregation directly into the overflow of His spirit, and opens the Bible, reads the Word, and teaches in ways that change your life! Ask yourself, are they really teaching about the life and works of the Lord and Savior Jesus Christ? Or, are they teaching their own life and works?

> "Herein lies the great subtleness of the devil. As long as there is an altar call, everything appears to be scriptural. Let them come...as long as they don't receive Jesus as their Savior, everything is fine. They can receive Jesus as a comforter of sorrows...a debt eliminator, a great friend...just as long as they DON'T RECEIVE HIM AS THE ONE WHO CAN SET THEM FREE!" (Oliver Greene, Acts of the Apostles Commentary, vol. 3)

Again, the damsel in Acts 16 is one example of someone demon-possessed, saying the right things for the wrong reasons; to deceive. The devil comes with a Bible in his hand. The devil preaches from the pulpit using the Bible. He used scripture to tempt Jesus in the wilderness. He twists and distorts the Word of God. He will use these kind of people to make you question the Bible and your own personal faith in the Lord Jesus Christ.

Protecting yourself against hermeneutical witchcraft and intellectual domination

1. First, recall the full armor from the previous chapters and the strategies for fighting. This may be a good time to reread the recommendations from the previous chapter.

2. Hide the Word in your heart! By reading it, studying it, understanding it, and mixing it with faith, it is ready for your use on every occasion.

3. Use the Word of God as your ultimate authority. Regardless of what man says, if it does not agree with the Word of God, discount and disregard it as counterfeit authority. Be careful, because this will not be a popular stance.

Personal Reflections:

My experience, of course, is in the predominantly "black church" where the influence of hermeneutic trickery prevails strongly. Many church leaders are skilled at the poetic voice and linguistic excellence necessary to wow unsuspecting members. Our encouragement to you, "Study to shew thyself approved!" There is no need for any parishioner to feel intellectually dominated. This is a direct play on the esteem of others and on the mind of the less trained. A ploy unfortunately used far too often in today's church.

1. How much time do you spend studying the Word of God?

2. When the preacher gives the scripture and verse, do you make notes so that you can read later, using your own Bible study tools?

3. Are you in a church that really examines the Word of God, or does your church specialize in messages that make you feel good?

CHAPTER EIGHT

LEGALISTIC CONTROL
(CAUGHT UP IN THE SYSTEM!)

"But their minds remain dull, for to this day the same veil remains when the old covenant is read. It has not been removed, because only in Christ is it taken away."
(2 Corinthians 3:14, NIV)

Paul's concern in his second letter to the church in Corinth was about the blatant disregard of the Corinthians towards the new covenant relationship the believers were now afforded. There were many divisions among the church. Some were glorifying in their own fornications and sins, some were desperately holding onto the Law of Moses, others were celebrating grace through Jesus Christ. Paul wanted badly for the believers of this day to conform to the joy found in living in Christ. Many had been *around* Him; the challenge now would be to *live in* Him.

So, Paul points out the blindness of Israel. Not only were the Israelites of Moses' time blinded, but the Jews in the time of Paul's letter had their minds so blinded that they could not behold the glory of the gospel. This is not referring to the same veil that was on Moses' face, but the veil of darkness and ignorance that had plagued the hearts and minds of the Jews. They no longer had to live by the law but accepted life as though they did!

There are many Christians who make a law of Christ Himself and His church, and think of their relationship and service to Him as an obligation. In so doing, they miss the loving and transforming nature of His words, His will and His ways. And so their minds remain dull because they have not experienced Christ in such a way as to move from just being *around* Him to living *in* Him. Apart from living in Him, we are governed then by the rules around us. We are not acquainted with life "apart from the system" and are therefore bound to satisfy the law within the system and are consequently found under condemnation.

Religious legalism seeks to manipulate and control others by the enforcing of often unspoken rules. These rules are an attempt to force behavior or action through condemnation or control tactics and present a direct contrast to a healthy fellowship of believers. The so-called Moses Principle, rule by one pastor, is favorable to some. Many people actually enjoy being controlled and dominated by church leaders. Their idea of "shepherding" is when all your personal decisions are made for you. Many others are unable to abide by these rules and doctrines and if they do not leave these situations, become spiritually dead and insensitive to their need to grow. They disconnect from the family they force themselves to live with and as a result, disconnect from their faith and their future. The sad things about this is that many are in this process and don't even know it!

Fellowship should bring peace and joy. Shepherds should lead us beside still water. They should not be the cause for personal and spiritual upheaval. As we grow in our faith, we should be more at peace. Mandated control does not lead to peace. Living in Christ leads to peace! Imposed unrealistic rules and restrictions lead to poor emotional, spiritual and physical health. Living as recipients of the new covenant of Jesus Christ leads to prosperity in our minds, bodies and our souls. Any imposition that leads to guilt and condemnation, as opposed to conviction and repentance, is not healthy faith. *"Therefore, there is now no condemnation for those who are in Christ Jesus, because through Christ Jesus the law of the Spirit of life set me free from the law of sin and death"* (Romans 8:1, NIV). Obedience, morality, conformity and generosity cannot be mandated, legislated or forced. They should be a natural manifestation of the influence of our faith upon us.

> *"It is for freedom that Christ has set us free. Stand firm then, and do not let yourselves be burdened again by a yoke of slavery."* (Galatians 5:1, NIV)

Legalistic control is defined here as using the laws and rules of the organization manipulatively, holding onto the letter of the law and forgetting the spirit. It can also include being selective about policies and procedures, using them to your benefit, at the expense of the follower. Primarily, legalistic control is abusing power, but within the auspices of the "proper way of doing things". When persons with counterfeit authority refer to structure and policy when they feel that their personal authority and territory are threatened they are engaging in legalistic control. Legalistic control is being manipulated and controlled by the law. It is in fact, the absence of grace.

When crack cocaine hit the streets in the mid '80s, it was the poor man's "coke". Powder cocaine had been popularized by businessmen, well-off college students, and entertainers for years. It had been sniffed, snorted, even injected, but not smoked. Pure cocaine was too expensive for the average person. And, the properties were not nearly as powerful or addictive as the rock, crack cocaine. Both are cocaine, yet the law has historically responded differently to users of powder vs. crack. Crack users are more likely to be arrested for possession, more likely to spend time in jail, and more likely to be classified as addicts. The laws on the street are not fair. Persons addicted to crack learn early that if you are pregnant and the baby is exposed to cocaine *in utero*, your child will automatically be taken and placed in foster care in some states. If you have one child in care, the burden of proof is on you that you are able to care for your other children, in other states. Moreover, the activities that surround supporting a crack habit involve breaking the law through crimes such as solicitation, prostitution, bad checks, possession, theft, sexual battery. These are crimes prevalent among these persons addicted to crack cocaine. Not so for powder coke addicts. Some lawyer is present who recommends an expensive drug treatment/spa facility and the record is expunged with some well-intentioned community service. If the addict is an ethnic minority, chances are if they are arrested they will do some time in the county jail or state penitentiary. An addict's survival depends on his or her ability to maneuver around the legal system. Ms. M described a time when she was arrested:

> "I remember one time a guy wrote a check and he talked me into going to cashing the check in the bank and I went in there and somehow they knew it was a bad check. I tried to run. The police threw me down in the parking lot. I've been to jail quite a few times. Jail didn't bother me. I could get some rest. I would be ready to go back again."

Ms. M had gotten to the point in her addiction where the law became her savior, or so it seemed. For most, the aftermath of having a criminal record, or, having to satisfy conditions of probation or parole, makes life difficult for years to come. The law may be their short-term salvation, but their enemy in the long run. With every job application, every application for a loan, every application to school or college, the prayer of the former addict is for grace from the powers that be.

How does legalism work manipulatively in the church? Religious legalism is the strict imposition of "religious" rules, laws, polices created by individuals, groups, or institutions in order to maintain order and control over individuals, groups, and processes. Legalistic control is when those laws are used manipulatively.

> "Much of the abusive manipulation in the corporate church today stems from the desire to build large, powerful ministries or to bring others under their control in

order to maintain the excesses of the church business and its leadership." (Jack Porcello, *Legalism Recovery*)

The checklist below was adapted from Porcello and is illustrative of some signs to be on the lookout for to determine if you might be a victim or perpetrator of legalistic control in your church. Before reading the checklist, you may already have your suspicions. Does it seem that the rules of the church are unpredictable? Do you sense an absence of grace? Does your church foster a climate where it is alright to be imperfect or to even fail? You should be in a church where the rules are predictably applied without respect of persons; grace should be apparent; and the climate should be where it is perfectly acceptable to try and fail. The Word says in Proverbs 24:16, *a just man falleth seven times, and riseth up again: but the wicked shall fall into mischief.*

Signs Of a Legalistic Ministry
(adapted from Porcello, but examples are mine):

✓ All policies are set and decisions made by one person or a small elitist group.

For example, in my situation, there was always a very small group of people who made ALL the decisions for the church. The input of "lay people" served only as an appeasement for the sake of the morale of ministry. Every final decision was made by very few people, and this group literally ran the church. They were afforded different privileges. They were allowed a different set of rules. They were the elite!

✓ Improprieties of church leadership are covered up, and those who question them are vilified.

In my experience, the culture of silence serves as a sort of private code of communication. One daren't do or say anything, unless it is to cover any wrongdoings and are committed to silence thereafter. It was a painful reality, and it often feels as though one is "aiding and abetting".

✓ Suggestions from the members are ignored or dismissed by church leadership.

From the 18 years of my experience, unless you were of the elite group, your suggestions meant absolutely nothing! The problem was, the people never knew that!

✓ Undue financial requirements are enforced upon the membership (tithing, pledges, disclosure of private financial records).

An area of great concern throughout the body of Christ and a major topic of conversation will always surround giving. The number of pledges, the disclosure of financial records, and the appropriation of funds in my past were always a concern for the people. Right, wrong or indifferent, the financial matters of the church seemed to always leave a sore spot with the members. As a leader, I understand that tithing is biblical. Giving is a spiritual concept and I have always been obedient to it. The caution for leadership is that giving must always be based on a sound biblical foundation and leaders must remain honest about the appropriation of funds.

✓ Special preference is given to the wealthy and powerful, and to those who make large contributions to the church or church staff.

I can recall, after having given all that we were able, the feeling of disconnect when my family was not considered a "significant contributor". A special breakfast was held in honor of these elite, honoring their contributions to the exclusion of many. It did not sit well with 99% of the congregation, but again, we were sworn to a culture of silence and our "agreement" had to be demonstrated by the appearance of acceptance.

✓ Church spending and salaries of church staff are not disclosed in full detail.

The policy of many churches is to leave salaries of senior staff undisclosed. I recall a time when one member of my former church had the nerve to ask! He was discredited from that day forward. The business of that church was always delivered with very selective exposure.

✓ Financial statements are not openly shared with congregation.

A pastor has to balance what should be confidential and private, so I understand the necessity for privacy, but blatant cover-ups and the deliberate misrepresentation of spending is wrong and does not benefit the church at all. I have witnessed the manipulation of information. It is amazing the skill involved in "twisting" truth. Having lived through the murmuring caused by so many secrets, my leadership style is to tell it all!

✓ Statements are used to invoke guilt and shame, manipulating members to contribute to the support of certain projects.

This involved the hermeneutic mastery used to manipulate people into doing whatever you need them to do. Leaders should be influential people. They should have the ability to convey a point. They should be skilled in communication and well-versed at delivery. However, when that skill is used to manipulate and literally sway people into unethical practices, it is dead wrong! When people are made to feel guilty and shameful for their "shortcomings" as opposed to being encouraged for their willingness to even participate, the heart can grow weary of demands and thus shut down on any further participation. This is certainly not what church leaders are after.

✓ Special behaviors reflect "deeper spiritual experience" (e.g. speaking in tongues, visions, prosperity, health).

I have been in churches where certain gifts reflected deeper spirituality, only to discover that behind these gifts was no character development or likeness to Christ at all!

✓ Difficult conditions are attributed to "spiritual weakness" (e.g. sickness, poverty, doubt).

There was once a lady in the church, a minister, who would always tell the people if they were experiencing difficulties, it was because they weren't living right. Quite the contrary, if we are suffering, we are in good company! Jesus said that His disciples would suffer because He suffered. And, He learned obedience through the things that He suffered. In this case it wasn't the pastor but a leader who represented the pastor. Equally as dangerous! Pastors must be aware of what their frontline leadership is conveying to the people.

✓ The Church is standing rigidly against unrealistic behavioral demands (no dancing, no drinking, no smoking, hair length, specific dress, no card playing, etc.).

One of the specific areas of concern for me was the unspoken but known rule regarding the length of a boy's hair as it pertained to his ability to serve. In that ministry, they were not only forbidden to serve if their hair was a certain style, but they were made to feel as though they "missed the mark" as a result. The danger here is that this is an opinion and is not biblical. Respectfully I asked once for my leader to show me in scripture where one was not permitted to serve because of the style of his hair. I was told, "That's my word and that's the rule in THIS house."

✓ Constant feelings of anxiety and insecurity are present due to not being able to abide by these rules.

Right, wrong or indifferent, there were many and will be many who come in and out of churches for one reason or the other. That's understood. However, when people are made to feel like there is something "wrong" with them because they chose not to abide by these "unspoken rules", that's a form of spiritual abuse that is not acceptable. People should be able to make conscious choices about where they worship and about where they will serve. If that choice is not "your" church, that doesn't make them wrong; their leaving makes them honest!

✓ Church or ministry leaders are unable to accept when they make bad decisions.

In my 18 years of service, I NEVER saw or heard an apology from Senior Leadership. Knowing that all have sinned and come short, at some point, EVERY leader will make a bad decision or will fall. In such cases, leaders must be seen taking responsibility for their actions. They must be seen repenting. They must be seen forgiving. These are the examples of Christ that "make" disciples. When leaders do not accept their wrongs, neither will members!

The inability to accept error always leads one to find a scapegoat. Somebody has to be to blame! I'd seen others made example of but not until I was used in that way did I realize the nature of this demon and the darkness that it travels in. When the finances of my area of leadership were put under scrutiny and my staff served to correct it, the church experienced a deficit. I was then dismissed, and so I was blamed for the deficit. In this type of system, it is important to note that they are operated exclusively by the elite group. In this case, it was impossible for anyone "outside" the group to ever cause any financial harm to the institution. The parameters were all controlled. The spending was all controlled. Yet, to the congregation of "lay people", all these leaders were the cause of the financial hardships of the church. If they would only recognize the pattern!

✓ Elitism ("Our church is the only true church ." "No other group is as good as ours—all other groups are dead!")

As God began to elevate me in my personal ministry, I began to travel and meet other fellowships. Wonderful fellowships! I'd be excited to return and report to my leader of what I had learned and been exposed to. I discovered, that though he pretended to listen and be supportive, all the time he was very critical and demeaning towards any other leaders and churches that were not his own.

If your experience with a church, ministry, or church leader can be described by any of the list above, and you are feeling alienated, taken advantage of, or inadequate, you may be involved in a church under legalistic control. You may want to attempt confronting the issue with church or ministry leaders, and try to reconcile the situation. If that doesn't work out, you may want to consider finding another church or ministry group.

It should be noted that not everyone is uncomfortable with following rules blindly. Some are intentionally seeking the structure of a system, because structure was missing in their home life or they grew up in militaristic systems with stringent hierarchies that no one dared to question. If that is you, then I challenge you to discover why these tactics are comfortable. I did. One of the things that kept me from confronting and exposing truth or some of the things that may have kept me from coming out earlier than I did was fear—fear of being rejected; of no longer being needed; and of no longer having this group. One of the things about addiction that makes the addiction more or less severe, is the length of time one is using. So if you stay in something long enough, the devil gets his talons in you and it's extremely difficult to break free. So, I don't take lightly that just because people have revelation knowledge they are easily able to just get up and walk out. It's deeper and more drastic than that and it has lasting consequences. I talk about this later in chapter nine.

For example, as my research will indicate, and based on my own experience, I have watched people for over 15 years— come to revelation knowledge and say, "I've got to break free." These were people not sitting on back rows, but were people with major roles in the church, including assistant pastors. You know you are under legalistic control when you see great, godly, influential leaders in a church torn down, because they are responding to the call of God to do something different. It is not uncommon to hear from church leadership just how wrong they are or how insignificant they are or how God did not tell them to do what God told them to do.

When you watch leadership respond to the call of God on their lives, leaders who have been instrumental in the birth, growth, development and the on-going operations of the ministry—when you watch people like that leave a church and nothing is said about them except how bad, ugly and dark they are and how worthless and meaningless and how punitive their lives should be—when you hear those kinds of things, it can invoke fear even in those who are sitting and serving and trying to do the right thing. So, it is easy to conform to the culture of silence and simply follow the rules.

Jesus raised the disciples to send them out—this is a key point. Jesus had a multiplying effect on ministry—that's what He intended to do. He trained them to send them out. In my case, and in cases all across this country, where a church is almost 20 years old, and not one person who has gone has ever been sent, I think that is an indication that there is a major problem. This does not line up with scripture. Of the many gifted, well-trained, high-impact people, who made significant differences in the life of the ministry, it is tragic that the majority left and none were sent.

So, here I sat watching, saying, "God I'm working too hard not to leave right." Only to discover that I had to push my own envelope just to get an announcement that I was leaving. Only to discover that the moment I stepped out the door my name would become mud. The same Julia McMillan who was so valuable yesterday, all of a sudden is the scum of the earth tomorrow.

We see this same situation on Palm Sunday on the triumphal entry of Jesus when He came riding in on the donkey (read Luke 19:35-38). The operative praise is Hosanna—today He's Hosanna, glory be to God in the Highest, but within four and a half days the same Jesus would be called to crucifixion, and the same people who were cheering for Him would be shouting for His death by crucifixion.

The interesting thing about this is some of those addicted in the pew have the courage to get free. I'm one of those people. My courage came from not trying to make a mark in the ministry, but my courage came when I looked at my own life and paralleled it to the life of Jesus Christ. So if Jesus could be cheered for on Sunday and cursed on Thursday, then so can I. I found myself in good company, so that's why I got up, packed my bags, did what I was supposed to do and let Jesus escort me out.

To God be the glory!! Legalistic control, supported by the fear of being rejected and the fear of being cursed and the fear of being talked about and the fear of being ostracized—those are tricks of the enemy, and I have come and written this book to tear that demonic kingdom down.

It is important to note that the same folks who were standing along the streets cheering for Jesus were cheering for Him because they had revelation knowledge that He was indeed the Messiah. They were cheering for Him because they knew their help had finally come. Many of them had been healed by Him, many of them had been taught by Him, many of them had been delivered by Him, many of them had been helped by Him and many of them had been "hoped" by him.

Likened to Jesus Christ, the same people who ostracized and called me everything but a child of God are the same people who had been helped by me, had benefitted from my ministry, been loved by me, been lifted by me, liberated by me, kept in the ministry by me—so guess what, I'm in good company, and if you find yourself reading this book and you can identify with what I'm talking about, then so are you.

I was in the grip of legalism, with no grace. People were watching how often and what time I reported to my job, though given permission to begin another work assignment. Paychecks were garnished without notice or discussion of missed time. Demands to teach on the teaching schedule were suddenly the priority and required of all ministers. Others were silenced from preaching when rules were not followed. All leaders were instructed to report and sign-in to leadership meetings so that absenteeism could be counted as the absence of a true call. Budget shifted without notice, depending on what the money was needed for. No disagreements or disputes among senior staff were allowed. Even the most difficult personnel must be accepted and made comfortable. Yes, even love was legislated!! Breaking the rules meant the loss of privileges, being silenced, being subjected to verbal tirades and threats. People are often afraid to walk away from situations where they are being controlled. The idea of change can be frightening. The consequences are both real and imagined. These steps are designed to help the "addict" who might be caught up in this type of abuse.

Protecting Yourself from Legalistic control and Systemic Domination

1. Recognize that the problem is in the system and that you are not to blame.

Those who abuse positions and power in ministry are the problem.

Many become involved in ministry to lord over others. Some have been instructed poorly, and are in bondage themselves. Others confuse personal convictions with divine guidance for the ministry. In each of these cases, these are ministers who need help, not obedience from addicts in the pews. It is natural to be angry in these situations, but remember that the anger will subside as the healing process begins. (Porcello)

2. Decide to be free from undue guilt and shame.

   Each time feelings of guilt, shame, and condemnation arise, they must be met squarely with the gospel.

3. Read the book of Romans and know what the Word says about law and grace. (Start with Romans 6:14, you are not under law, but under grace!)

Since man is imperfect and man created religion as a set of guidelines to worship God, religion is imperfect. In some churches, these guidelines become laws, or rather doctrine, that the congregation is expected to follow. Religions often use biblical scripture in order to back up these doctrines and laws. Most of the time it is through the interpretation and misinterpretation of the Bible that these laws become reality to the members. In the process of establishing and enforcing these "man-made rules and doctrines", the church leadership becomes no better than modern-day Pharisees. This eventually can drive people away from Christianity, which is the ultimate sin. In their attempt at cultivating a flock, they have driven people away. (Porcello)

Pharisees were known for their so-called knowledge of the law of Moses, and made rules to assist the law of Moses in governing God's people. Jesus called them blind guides. They made rules that they themselves could not follow. And, Jesus predicted that they would not receive the blessings of God because of it. In the gospel of Matthew, Jesus speaks directly to the Pharisees using an indicting seven woes. The woes had to do with them performing hypocritically, with counterfeit authority, thus leading people astray. The thing that was most disconcerting about these leaders was that they gave traditional interpretations of the teachings of man equal authority with the Old Testament teachings of Moses. When the scripture did not agree with what they were teaching, they promoted their own teachings. Not only did they require others to follow their teachings, but they themselves were hypocritical about following.

"Woe to you, teachers of the law and Pharisees, you hypocrites! You shut the kingdom of heaven in men's faces. You yourselves do not enter, nor will you let those enter who are trying to. (Matthew 23:13)

The spirit of Pharisees is alive and well in the church today in the form of legalistic control. Authoritarianism, a demand for unqualified submission to authority, without allowing the freedom of thinking for oneself, is a sure trap for legalistic control. Power corrupts. And, corruption can and does exist in the church leadership. Ministers and high church officials are no better or worse than the individual church members. The reality is that all are imperfect and fall short.

"Unfortunately, these Legalistic churches are wide spread. Their membership is strong and their corrupt behavior will continue. The children and adults will continue to suffer at the hands of church leadership. The man-made doctrine will continue. And the sinful behavior of the pastors and church leadership may not stop. Perhaps some will read this and will reevaluate their religion and break free of the tyranny that exists. And, hopefully, the ones that are out there and hurting will be able to find a good, honest Christian church that can minister to their individual needs and wants. One must go where the spirit leads them." (Porcello)

In the world of drugs, the rules are most pronounced between the supplier and the middle man. There is an intricate system of rules and ethics for moving the drug. Deviations from the rules can create undue exposure and vulnerability to law enforcement encounters. An addict will turn any trick for the pusher. The pusher becomes his or her savior, making manipulation and coerced cooperation easy. The pusher keeps pushing until the addict burns out or dies, but he survives by lining up new victims. And so it is with the church addict. It is the staff that suffers most from the intricate system of unwritten rules, and hypocritical ethics. Deviation from the rules creates undue exposure of the pastor to members or oversight bodies. The pastor who practices legalistic control keeps pushing until the addict burns out or dies, and he quickly replaces him or her with a fresh victim.

Personal Reflections:

The people perish for lack of knowledge! If you are in a church system and these characteristics are familiar to you, you may wish to sit with your leader and begin to ask pertinent questions. Make a decision for yourself or your family that will cause you to disconnect from this type of organization. Take it from one who knows, it is dangerous, it is deceptive and it is destructive!

1. How honest were you when completing the checklist?

2. Did you learn something that requires a prayerful response?

CHAPTER NINE

THE POWER OF THE BLACK LIGHT
(ILLUMINATION / REVELATION)

"What is the way to the abode of light? And where does darkness reside?" (Job 38:19) (NIV)

Out of a mighty storm, God speaks. Out of miry clay, God lifts. Out of darkness, God brings forth light. Although He had not answered any of Job's questions, nor responded to any of Job's emotions, God yet leads and guides. Job's questions and his circumstance were not at the heart of the issue for God. The heart of the issue for God was to reveal Job's ignorance of that which operated in the natural. Job was a distraught man because he did not understand the workings of God's physical creation. If he could not understand the workings of God's physical creation, how could he possibly understand God's mind and character? There is but one standard for us to live by and that's God Himself. Our only option is to submit to His sovereignty and authority and to rest solely in His care.

God was reserving for Job that which He had planned for him but there would be a prerequisite! Job had to first understand that his life was not to be governed by material things, temporary happiness or the prince of darkness of this world. He would become a man of complete reverence to God who would live by his own words: *"Naked I came from my mother's womb, and naked will I depart. The Lord gave and the Lord has taken away; may the name of the Lord be praised"* (Job 1:21) (NIV).

Job recognized his brokenness and could therefore begin his recovery. A common echo of families of addicted people is that they will only begin to recover when they themselves see that there is a problem. Job had to *see*! Not through the naked eye but through spiritual eyes. So many people in the modern church view life through the naked eye. God wants us to see through our spiritual eyes and in most cases, that will mean that our dark places must be exposed. *"Have nothing to do with the fruitless deeds of darkness, but rather expose them"* (Ephesians 5:11) (NIV). Many parishioners remain in darkness not because they cannot see, but because they do not wish to be exposed. Freedom in God is not a geographic location; it is an inward revelation that in Christ we are made free. We are made free because He came to bear our sins and to shed us of our shame. There is no guilt in God. There is no shame in Christ. Past sins have been forgiven. He is always making us new!

Job had to hit rock bottom before he could see! He had to see that through all his pain and heartache, God had purpose attached to it. God never forgot about Job. "He knows our frame, He remembers that we are dust" (Psalm 103:14, NIV).

Even in the midst of rock bottom moments, God knows how to illuminate the situation. God knows what we can handle and what we cannot. He is the author and the finisher of our faith and as such, He is the One who can respond to our brokenness and restore our frame!

How do many sit in churches under the pretense of fellowship? How do many sit under the absence of the Spirit? How do many avoid the painful but necessary steps of repentance and reconciliation? Because they have not experienced the Power of the Black Light.

God uses the power of the Black Light to expose us to the realities of our lives that we might begin the road to recovery. Revelation and information is given for application and restoration. Oh the joy of real freedom in God...but not before the power of the Black Light can invade our darkness and transfer us into His marvelous light. Let's investigate the Power of the Black Light!

In a forensic investigation such as one might see on popular nighttime dramas such as CSI and Cold Case, we see the use of ultraviolet light to illuminate the hidden evidence in a crime scene. This black light is powerful in that it reveals what cannot be seen by the naked eye. For example, it can reveal a hairline crack in an otherwise solid appearing metallic object. It can differentiate the real money from the counterfeit. It can reveal the presence of bodily fluids, such as blood, semen, or urine, even after the scene has been cleaned up. That which appears pristine and undisturbed can be the cradle of evidence of brokenness, violence, sexual assault, and of that which is counterfeit, when exposed to the black light.

Often times, when a person is addicted, they have lost sight of the place where their "normal" resides. Instead, they have normalized unbrushed teeth, uncombed hair, dirty clothes, bad breath, and indiscriminate sex. Some are known to say that they have gotten to a place where bad doesn't feel bad anymore. Then God allows something to happen that literally shines a black light on the addict, jolting the person to a conscious awareness that not only are they not normal, they are far from anything that looks, feels, thinks, or behaves like themselves. Who is this person who steals from their own family, walks the street in the wee hours of the morning to find a rock, lies down on the hard, filthy floors with strangers, trading sex for drugs, and smokes dope on the steps of the church? Who is this person who allows people to place fists in her face and guns to her head?

It was a difficult revelation for Ms. M to find herself with a mother's purse that contained the only money she had to buy toys for her children at Christmas. As she ran to escape those who were ready to kill her for the purse she had stolen, she came to herself. The black light began to shine, and she saw how low she had stooped. In fact, she had hit rock bottom. The revelation of what she had become brought her to her knees in a desperate plea to God, the only one who could save her. She could keep running or turn to face her accusers. She had nowhere to go, she had run out of excuses, rationalizations, and schemes. Only God could help her through this... She turned herself into the ones who chased her, begging for help, and there began the long road to recovery.

The road to recovery begins with the power of the black light that only seems to shine after the addict has found his or her bottom. That light is the revelation knowledge that one has a problem that only God can solve.

"We admitted we are powerless over our addiction and that our lives have become unmanageable without God.

The halls of AA meeting rooms ring loudly with this first and second step… face your addiction…come out of denial. The Apostle Paul says it this way:

"I know nothing good lives in me, that is, in my sinful nature. For I have the desire to do what is good, but I cannot carry it out." (Romans 7:18)

Paul had a problem that only God could solve. The same can be said of Job. After living with his condition of being on the brink of total destruction, one well-meaning friend attempted to speak truth about how God operates. Over and over again, God pulls our soul back from destruction, until we not only see the light, but begin to walk therein. The first act of recovery is to see the light. It is a mental act of evaluating the situation with God's standards for your life, and seeing how far we fall short. "I want to do right, but I can't," says Paul.

The addict in the pew is no different from Ms. M. The hitting bottom feels the same emotionally—there is a problem here that only God can solve. I cannot continue to worship or serve as a religious ritual. I am no longer growing from the food that is being served in this house. Like a stagnant body of water, I have sat on gifts much too long. I am dying a slow death, and no one seems invested in my life. In fact, I am totally engulfed in the toxicity of the messages, the relationships, and the hype. I have lost too much dignity, self-worth, confidence, and time. The black light shining on me reveals that I have become one who is also toxic and one who at times spreads the toxicity of the institution. I need God to intervene.

I (Julia McMillan) declare that I did not know that I was dying the dreadful death of an addict in the pew, until I was exposed to the living. It was in the presence of the living vessels, concerned more about my purpose in the kingdom than my personality or productivity in an institution, that the light penetrated my soul. These men and women, experienced in the path that I would one day walk, held up the black light began to illuminate areas of my brokenness, and then with the brilliant light of the Lord, began to slowly lead me to my healing.

The black light is used to expose that which has caused death. The black light is used to expose blood and fingerprints—to trace the perpetrator. I'm so glad God has some black lights in the Kingdom. I call them Ecclesiastical police.

There are some folks who are in pulpits across this country who are gifted with discernment and gifted with the ability to see beyond what the natural eye can see. The question becomes, "Who turned on the black light in my life?" God has stationed some people who are so gifted they don't have to talk about the problem; they are solution-oriented. They preach and teach the unadulterated, uncompromised, unhindered Word of God. They have pit bull tenacity about the things of God, and they are not in it to be compromised by any manipulating, dominating, controlling spirits. I was fortunate in my own life for my path to cross the paths of two great women of

God with such characteristics, and many men and women in ministry throughout this country. Every now and then, a word would fall down in my spirit that would bring about change and illumination; spirit and life that I so desperately needed.

The problem in the body of Christ and the primary theme of this book is that many church goers are addicts in pews, who sit with a false interpretation of what spiritual life really is. The Bible warns us in John 10: 10 that "the thief comes to kill, steal, and destroy but I have come to that you might have life and that more abundantly". And so, God would use humans on the earth to speak life into that which is dead. Just like the black light, the Word comes to expose sin. And, the thing I love about God and laugh about concerning the enemy is that the enemy leaves his fingerprints on stuff he should have never touched.

So they come to expose where the enemy has been and trace the nasty mess he has made and yes even the murder(s) he has committed. There is no doubt that spiritual deaths have been caused by perpetrators of charismatic witchcraft, hermeneutic manipulation, and legalistic control. Ironically and tragically, there are times when the only people who don't know they are guilty are the perpetrators. You can even show the perpetrators proof and they will deny it. You can also speak truth and they will deny it. You can show it to them at the scene of the murder and they will deny it was them. So, I thank God for the black lights in my life that have come to illuminate that which is wrong.

Black lights not only come to expose that which is bad but to also expose that which is good. The exposure is not usually about minor personality quirks, but the exposure uses the Word of God and the Truth of God to illuminate dark recesses and crevices in my life. The black lights in my life have caused me to recognize that even though I was spiritually dying and in many places spiritually dead, there was life yet to be breathed into me because these words that [He] speaks are spirit and they are light. And though I was addicted, there was hope for recovery and a new dawn in my life.

The Bible tells us that there will be those who enjoy their darkness because they love their evil deeds (John 3:19). They don't want to be exposed and don't want to be corrected. Also, I'm reminded of the Proverb 16:2, used earlier in chapter 5 that says "there is a way a man thinketh himself right but his end is destruction". So, the Word of God comes to expose the foolishness that many of us see in pulpits today. However, persons must be open and receptive to the light of the Holy Spirit.

True illumination is the work of the Holy Spirit to search our hearts even in its most hidden recesses, to expose, and eradicate those things that are not suitable for His purposes for you; even those hidden motives that you have held secret, and those deep desires that only He can satisfy. His desire is to clear a direct path for you to hear and receive His unique call for your life that only He can bring to fruition.

Overcoming an addiction may be the most challenging confrontation endured in one's life. Whether the addiction is a substance or to spiritual authority, it will involve the same processes. Just look up any online source for how to recover from an addiction, and you will find similar suggestions:

Step 1—You must admit that there is a problem. It matters not whether it pertains to drugs or alcohol or with spiritual and emotional authority. You may have to reluctantly admit that you are an addict. Moving out of denial has to be the first step. Without this there is no chance of recovery.

Church life gone askew is particularly difficult to recover from because so much is tied to the perception of our relationship with God and what He has said and not said, ordained and not ordained. Church folk intentionally dress up, cover up, stand up, and appear to be righteously motivated, even when they are falling apart at the seams. How much courage does it take for a dressed up, "fessed-up" saint to shine a light that might expose duplicity (double-mindedness), phoniness, resentment, and even pain or shame? How much courage does it take to not smile when others smile or say amen when others do, when your insides have already begun to say, this is not me, I must move on? One must move out of denial and into the necessity of facing the situation....As we say in our church, "It Is What It Is!"

Step 2 - Decide if you're willing to do whatever it takes to succeed at recovery. This can be one of the most painful areas of recovery; having the courage to take responsibility for one's own life. As it pertains to the church, having the courage to trust God at His words and believing that the promises of God pertain not only to misguided, unconcerned, or reprobate church leaders, but to you as well! "God grant me the serenity to accept the things I cannot change, Courage to change the things I can, and the Wisdom to know the difference!"

Step 3 - Be ready and willing to change everything in your life - friends, hangouts, beliefs, habits, churches, thoughts about yourself. ...BE WILLING TO DETACH! I address physical separation in my next chapter, but before it is possible to detach, you must fix your mind on the possibility. In other words, imagine yourself away from the familiar...God is about to do a new thing, if you let Him have His way.

Step 4 - Connect with the appropriate source of help. If the addiction is substance abuse, connect with Alcoholics Anonymous, Narcotics Anonymous, Cocaine Anonymous, Marijuana Anonymous - whichever one best serves your needs. You will need this support and fellowship. If the addiction is an unhealthy or unproductive fellowship, seek God's direction for a healthy one and one that carries a mandate for restoration and recovery.

At first, abstaining from an addiction that has controlled the mind, body, soul, and spirit for so long does make us feel insecure and self doubting, but there is hope. The addict can endure and overcome those fears through the help of God. But before any of this will have any real impact on the addict, he or she must want to quit the addiction!!

"By trusting in what God says is true, you can believe in the power of God's words to help guide you away from your fears and into God's truth and love. God's words are the addicts comfort and refuge. God's breath-filled words, and spiritual presence over-powers evil and reveals the truth in the addict. The evil is the addiction, and God's loving kindness is stronger and more powerful than any addiction." (Angie Lewis, 2005, Overcoming Addiction)

God will shine the light; the addicted must respond!

Personal Reflections:

In a meeting during the summer of 1996, an awesome woman of God preached a message entitled, "Obedience in the Inward Regions". I'd never been challenged in the private places of my life. It was as though I had been pierced with exposure. The Lord sent His mouthpiece to me, directly for me, and her words penetrated the hell out of me....literally! I began to seek God for my healing and deliverance. He led me to the right people for my help. He "caused" me to triumph. At the revelation knowledge of the Black Light, I decided to make a change. I decided that the life of cover up was no longer for me. My prayer for you as you read this book is that the same God who sent rescue to me, will do the same for you. He WILL illuminate....will YOU respond?

CHAPTER TEN

BREAKING THE VICIOUS CYCLE
(I QUIT!)

"Thus says the Lord: "In a time of favor I have answered you; in a day of salvation I have helped you; I will keep you and give you as a covenant to the people, to establish the land, to apportion the desolate heritages, saying to the prisoners, 'Come out,' to those who are in darkness, 'Appear.' They shall feed along the ways; on all bare heights shall be their pasture" (Isaiah 49: 8—9).

There comes a time that becomes "the acceptable time"! In a time of favor, the Lord will answer us! Long before our Savior was born, God had chosen Him to bring light into a dark and sinful world. He had chosen Him to set the captives free. He had chosen Him to bring sight to the blind and to bring restoration to those who had been in bondage. He'd already ordained that His presence would not only illuminate darkness, but it would draw men unto Himself. With this ever present tug of the soul, comes an invitation: Come out!

I equate this to the old familiar game of hide-and-seek. We always liked to play this game in the dark. Why? Because the darkness seemed to provide a sense of cover...a sense of security in one's hiding...a sense of protection from the seeker. Our lives are no different. Darkness offers for many, a false sense of security, an illusion of safety.

At the first stage of the game, the seeker would actually give you time to hide! They would often count for an established period of time before pursuing you. There was a phrase that the seeker had to yell so that you knew that the pursuit had begun: "Ready or not...here I come!" and the search was on! I can hear these words coming from our Savior to all who are living in darkness, "Ready or not, here I come!" At the time of our scripture, the Messiah had not yet come, but here was a pronouncement to "come out to those who are in darkness: Appear!"

At some point in the game, the seeker would say to the hidden one, "Come out! Come out! Wherever you are! Ally Ally in come free!!!! At this point the message is clear. The game is over. The hiding is over. The darkness is over. The disconnect is over. The displacement is over....Come out! Come out! Wherever you are! And at this point, the hidden one must choose to appear!

Whether from drug abuse or spiritual abuse, one must choose to take his or her life back. The Narconon Freedom Center, one of the most successful drug treatment centers in the country, offers this encouragement:

> "Addiction is an equal opportunity destroyer that will take your goals, your self-esteem, your money, your family, your job, and eventually, your life. The good news is...you can have your life back!"

As strong as the hold of addiction can be, no matter how tight its grip, Christ in us is stronger than ANY addiction. Despite the level of difficulty, we have the ability to break that hold forever. Addiction has a beginning and so does recovery. Ironically enough, they both start at the same point—a choice!

> "Drug addiction is a cruel, merciless enemy. Once it has you cornered, it often seems there is no way out. What seemed like harmless recreational drug use became a prison of pain, guilt, shame, and hopelessness. Drug addiction operates under the "Frankenstein Theory": if you create the monster, you own it. No one deliberately makes a choice to become addicted to drugs, but we do make a choice about using drugs recreationally that ultimately led to addiction...your choice to take back what belongs to you; your life, your health, and your spirit. Things that you thought were gone forever can be restored if you make that choice and mean it."
> ("Breaking the Cycle"—Narconon Freedom Center)

An addict who decides to be clean and sober comes to him or herself, generally, when life seems like it cannot possibly get any worse. From a position of surrender, the addict looks up to God or to someone stronger than themselves and cries out for help. The cry may be a confession that I need treatment, and am willing to do whatever it takes to get into treatment. The bottom line is there are no more excuses. No reason is valid enough to delay the change that must occur. The time is now or never; do or die.

Ms. M knew as she was being held at gun-point waiting for the police to come that she was at the end of a long struggle.

The physical separation from the crack cocaine occurred in the jail cell. The mental separation would come through months of treatment. The entire human system is affected when one becomes an addict—bio-psycho-social-spiritual aspects of life are all impacted. The physical body needs time to recuperate from the constant infusion of a stimulant into the blood stream. This physical toll may have included heart disease, high blood pressure, nutritional issues, and the strange feelings of bugs crawling under the skin. Psychologically, the former addict may deal with depression that comes from knowing, in a sober state, the full extent of what has been lost. Normal relationships are strained, trust is broken, and anxiety and paranoia are high. Socially, an entire community of places, persons, and things, has shifted to keeping regular hours, sleeping and eating at predictable intervals, hanging out with people who do not use drugs. And spiritually, the absence of the drug makes room for spiritual growth. Now, instead of meeting at the crack house waiting for the pusher, the newly-committed recovering addict meets in the halls of an AA/NA meeting. Hello, my name is Ms. M, and I am a recovering crack addict!

Overnight, an entire community has shifted. The good-byes are emotional and encouraging from most. "You won't see me any more here (in the crack house), I'm going into treatment." The pusher is usually emotionless. "Go for it," he says, with false encouragement, with a smirk that says you probably will not make it. There is another person who has just become addicted to replace his sales. No time to reminisce. Good-bye and good luck. I hope you make it, with a smirk, and a shooing away.

As it parallels the church and the abuse of spiritual authority, just as the crack addict must "decide" to take his/her life back, so must the wounded parishioner. This is the time when the wounded are able to begin to appropriate the scriptures for their own lives. This is the time where reality sets in, "Oh! God speaks to me too!!!" This is the time when the written word becomes the living word! This is the time when we decide to transfer over for the promises to the manifestation of His words. This is the time! Then why is the "time" so difficult???"

Ron Henzel describes the difficulties of breaking free in his article entitled, "They Told Me That If I Left".

> "One of the most insidious features of spiritual abuse is the state of terror in which it leaves so many of its victims. People who flee spiritual abuse are in a doublebind: in the very process of fleeing from the oppression that comes from being part of the group, they are terrorized by the threats of the leadership and various members — threats of dire consequences, punishment from God, and even eternal damnation." (Henzel)

Have you heard rumors of what happens when people leave? I have. Like in the drug culture, the expectation from other addicts is that if you leave, you will find that your place is really in the crack house and you will soon return. Like drug culture, if you leave you are judged at times as thinking that you are somehow better than those left behind. When the truth is that God has given you a moment of lucidity and sobriety, enough to make a decision for a life of freedom and not bondage that leads to death.

If you leave, you will not make it on your own, and you will eventually return. If you leave, you will not prosper. If you leave, and others follow you, God will be displeased and your ministry will not be blessed. If you leave, you will miss the blessing of the former house. If you leave, you can be replaced, because you are not really needed. If you leave, you are not worthy of continued fellowship or support. And, the list goes on. Some of the threats were even more amazing to witness second-hand. One was told that if he left, he'd be prosecuted to the limit of the law! Another was told that if he left, the church that wanted him would regret it, because he wasn't "ready." Interestingly, I was told that when I left, I'd receive the "blessings and the bounty" of my church, the church that I'd served so faithfully in or nearly 20 years. All were lies!

Henzel quotes a favorite verse that spiritual abusers use in order to intimidate people: 1 John 2:16: *They went out from us, but they did not really belong to us. For if they had belonged to us, they would have remained with us; but their going showed that none of them belonged to us.*

The idea of ownership is important to both pushers in the streets and in pulpits. There is much discussion of taking other's "customers" or "members." It is rare that a mature Christian is given credit for following the leading of the Holy Spirit and making an assertive choice to leave one congregation for another that may be more suitable to their gifts or calling. The idea that one would break away in response to feeling spiritually abused is altogether unfathomable. If one leaves, it must be something wrong with them, not the organization or the people they are leaving.

> One by one, as members leave or are kicked out, their reputations are smeared and their characters are assassinated by the leader. Most of the time, the leader doesn't have to say hardly anything. The simple fact that he ordered someone to leave is enough to persuade the other members that the person is in some kind of sin. (Henzel, *They Told Me If I Left*)

One of the most difficult aspects of leaving is the paranoia one feels knowing that you become the topic of others, conversations/gossiping, and that a type of shunning is occurring. Suddenly, the persons who were once friendly to you do not return your call. The lunches you used to have with brothers or sisters from the former ministry are fewer and fewer between. There appears to be a slippery slope from a façade of "you are still ok with everyone in leadership" to "your contributions and participation in the church were meaningless, or worse, detrimental."

> Recovering from spiritual abuse is not simply recovering from a single issue, but recovering from a whole *complex* of issues that all connect to each other. It takes time to track down each one and disconnect it from your thinking, but over time you can do it. (Henzel)

Often a leader will go through a whole list of "warnings," similar to the ones listed above, and if those do not produce the desired response, the leader tells his flock, "Well, if we were *really* dealing with a Christian here, he or she would have listened to my warnings." When leaders become controlling enough to admonish your free choice from the pulpit in vague messages related to your personal choices, you have probably already missed your exit.

Are you ready to quit? The question is how do you disconnect? Well, I submit that disconnection takes place in three places and in three ways. One must disconnect first of all in their own mind. Once God has given revelation and the black light has come on. Now it is the duty of the addict to decide for his or her own life. One says to himself, " I recognize now that I am an addict; I recognize that I have been mislead; and now I must make a decision concerning myself." Many families of addicts grow weary in well doing because they believe the addict in their family should listen to their counsel and that they themselves have the power to speak life into the addicted family member. "You got to go get healed, you got to go get detoxed, you got to get cleaned, you need to do this, and you need to do that!" But, until that revelation belongs to the addict there will be no movement towards healing. And so I submit that the first area of disconnect is in the mind.

Often, the addict in the pew, having come to him or herself, wrestles with what to do about the revelation. For some, the reality is: "I'm not growing; I have lost my passion; I'm just going through the motions. Perhaps if I involve myself more, give more, join in with leadership more, this feeling of 'something is wrong' will go away. So they sit and submit—and the fleeting moments of clarity come fewer and farther between. Persons who are strong enough to resist the organizational pressure to stay and get involved, versus leave and be whole again, often find themselves having to take the most difficult stance ever taken in their lives—I WILL NO LONGER SUBMIT.

> "There are times when you should consciously REFUSE to submit to authority—if it is not based on God's authority. Silent, unquestioning obedience in the face of dishonesty and abuse will only enable that dishonesty and spiritual abuse to be passed on to the next generation. Blind submission must be REPLACED with responsible actions. Sometimes we are waiting for God to do what God is waiting for us to do!" (Joyner)

Mentally, one must come out of denial and recognize the putrid state he or she is in and stop submitting. Often times when we have great and charismatic leaders in our lives they become larger than life—like little gods. I am not suggesting that Uzziah was practicing witchcraft. We do know that he disobeyed God and went in the Temple when only priests were authorized to go in there. But I am suggesting that Uzziah was an idol in the life of Isaiah, and when King Uzziah died, that was also the year when Isaiah saw the Lord. And when one sees the Lord, he is not only expected to see the Lord, he is also expected to respond to the Lord. Therefore, in the words of Isaiah, I am a man of unclean lips and I am around a people of unclean lips.

What is interesting to note here about Isaiah, and it runs parallel to my own life, is that these words are spoken in Isaiah chapter six, but in Isaiah chapters one through five, Isaiah has been around these people of unclean lips and He has also been a prophet. So why is it that this prophet is speaking in five chapters and no one sees God until chapter six? In addition, he himself does not see God until chapter six. He has been speaking for five chapters but he does not see God until chapter six. Isn't it interesting that a prophet does not see God for the first chapters of his life. Working for the Lord, without a personal encounter, is surely a dangerous thing!

Isaiah's words were, "I am a man of unclean lips..." so he recognized the rotten state he was in. He recognized his condition. Therefore when one has a mental revelation of his or her state, he or she disconnects mentally from those who are surrounding him or her and that is exactly what I did. I saw myself through God's eyes and I heard my call clearer than ever before.

In the year 2000, when I began seminary, a fellow addict in the pew accused me in front of our pastor, saying, "Ever since Minister Julia started school she has not had anything to say to me." And I said, "That's good thing because when you respond to the call of God on your life, it minimizes conversation and it certainly minimizes the people in your life!" So, although I was still physically there at the former church, I was mentally disconnecting at that time. My fellow addicted "friend" helped me to see my mental disconnect more clearly and I thank her for that revelation to this day.

The second place one must disconnect is in one's spirit. Isaiah said "...I am a man of unclean lips..." And the Lord comes with the tongs from the altar and dispatches his Angels to clean him up. The Lord has not physically sent Isaiah out of his geographical location yet, but the Lord cleans him up. As soon as Isaiah gives the confession there is a cleansing. And when the cleansing happens with Isaiah, he has been washed, and Isaiah's spirit is no longer the same! Although Isaiah is positionally in the same location, he has been transferred by virtue of the cleansing that has taken place in his spirit. So there has already been a mental disconnect, and now, he experiences a disconnect in his spirit. Finally, there is a physical disconnect.

The Bible says God had been speaking to Isaiah. In verse eight of chapter six the Lord says whom shall I send? And the very next line the Lord says "Who shall go for us?" It moves from a singular to a plural. From the time of Isaiah's own acknowledgement, God had not only covered Isaiah by His sovereignty, but saved him from the state he was in and cleaned him up and postured him for service. Today's "Isaiahs" are covered by God, saved by the Son of Man, Jesus Christ, and are cleansed/sanctified by the Holy Spirit! Today we go in the name of the Father, the Son, and the Holy Spirit. We cannot do the work of the Lord until all three have infused our lives.

Let us now consider Isaiah's quick response: "Here am I Lord, send me." This response foretells a physical disconnect. I too would soon make this physical disconnect. The preparation was as painful as burning coals on lips of flesh, and as agonizing as the preparation was, I survived, and I quit!

Allow me to offer a personal example. Alcoholism has plagued my family down through the years. And I was no exception. I had picked up that seed and was running with it. But when I decided to disconnect mentally, spiritually, and physically from my drug of choice, I was able to break the vicious cycle, and quit. I believe Paul says in Galatians 5 "return no longer to that which once had you in bondage." I have not returned to alcohol, nor will I ever be an addict in the pew again.

Isaiah says it this way: *"Remember not the former things, nor consider the things of old. Behold, I am doing a new thing; now it springs forth, do you not perceive it? I will make a way in the wilderness and rivers in the desert"*(Isaiah 43:18-19).

Most who have decided to change church communities have undergone similar processes. Initially, they find every way to stay connected to the healthier aspects of the ministry they are leaving. They send encouraging messages to leadership, they attend major functions to support old friends in the former ministry, and they occasionally even leave a financial gift. Gradually, they begin to reduce their contact with members and leadership. The separation is painful to say the least. It fosters feelings of sadness, loneliness, guilt, shame, and anger. Remember, the person is not just losing relationships with individuals; they are losing the benefit of an entire community.

To disconnect is like going through a separation or divorce. It is hard to heal from broken relationships while still engaging in occasional intimacy. Most attempts at intimacy are false and futile attempts to hold on to or regenerate positive feelings that you already know have gone. Any prolonging of the physical and permanent separation causes a great paradox of being in limbo, and delays healing. The following is offered for your consideration after you have decided to quit.

1. Separate yourself completely, and give yourself time to hear from the Lord regarding where He is leading you. Fasting and praying will be helpful during this stage.

2. Seek Godly counsel from friends outside of the organization you are leaving.

3. Leave without apology: write a letter or make a phone call to the appropriate persons informing them of your decision to leave.

4. Don't deny negative emotions. Find a safe person to discuss the loss that you are experiencing, and the anger you may be steeped in as a result of the "witchcraft, manipulation, and control".

5. Do not connect to another fellowship, without investigating the dynamics of the leaders and of the organization. Remember, you are trying not to choose the same type of experience. Attend churches for Christian fellowship, but don't be pressured to make a choice right away.

6. Seek the "new thing" God has for you. Don't compromise. It is there! Like a stream in the desert it awaits your refreshing, renewal, and regeneration.

7. Forgive those who have wronged you. Forgiveness is a process that may require your revisiting the hurt from time to time to discern if you are letting go of anger, hurt, and resentment. A special note here: face the fact

that abuse hurts even the strongest of us. There is help for your hurts.

8. Enter the next fellowship/community knowing that you need a period of continued detoxification and healing. With God's help, seek to purify yourself as you are restored from an addiction or a toxic spiritual environment.

Personal Reflections:

Of the nearly 20 years of service at my former ministry, I witnessed over five top leaders leave. These were senior staff personnel, preachers, pastors, ministry leaders. These were people who had served faithfully with their time, talents and treasures. But each of them was ostracized, criticized and demoralized. I sat and wondered..."How could the same person who, yesterday, was such a valuable member of this team, all of a sudden today become an evil witch or imposter?" I would never receive answers. I began to ponder my own departure and I declared to myself and my pastor, I have served to long and too faithful to leave the wrong way. I had frequent conversations with him about my transition. I asked for help in planning it. I asked for guidance in executing it. I did all I knew to do. But for me, it was no different. He acted as though he was supportive...even made an announcement to the church (at my urging!). But I later discovered, my good work, and godly intentions did not matter to him. Little did I know, that as I watched the treatment of my brothers and sisters who left for whatever reasons, I was watching the treatment that would soon be mine. I would still become a scapegoat, morally raped, and ostracized. The people would be silent out of fear for their own positions, and the cycle of addiction in the pews would continue. To God be the Glory for breaking that vicious cycle in my life. It is what it is!

1. If you have considered quitting, what are you waiting for?

2. Is God glorified while you wait? Or, are you delaying a work that He has given you to do?

CHAPTER ELEVEN

THE NEED FOR DETOX
(RESTORATION FROM A TOXIC FAITH)

"Depart, depart, go out from there! Touch no unclean thing!
Come out from it and be pure, you who carry the vessels of the
Lord." (Isaiah 52:11, NIV)

Isaiah foretells a time when the remnant would come out of
Babylonian bondage and leave all unclean things behind—
especially the priests—those who carry the vessels of the Lord.

The Bible says that because of Jesus, we are now ALL priests
of God and as such, we are to remain clean (Rev. 1:6). These
are literally marching orders as God commands believers to
separate from that which is contaminated. He speaks specifically to those who bear the vessels of the Lord, meaning the
priests and Levites, those who carried the utensils of the
Temple. Part of the priests job was to "stay clean" so that he
could be used at anytime to work with "holy things".

I was reminded this week of how easy it is for that which is
clean to become defiled. I recently moved into a new home so
the areas of the house that are carpeted are at this time spotless! A worker entered the house after having been outside in

the dirt and grass. Stains and all, he stepped onto the white carpet. All of a sudden, that which had been spotless clean had become filthy! All because we did not take the necessary precautions to ward off the possibility of dirt meeting that which is clean. Now, it is interesting to note that if we had taken white carpet to the dirt, there would have been no transfer of cleanliness. However when we bring dirt to that which is clean, contamination is immediate!

People today have grown comfortable living toxic lifestyles. The food we eat is loaded with chemicals, the air we breathe is polluted, the conversations we engage in are contaminated, the churches we attend are toxic, the people we choose to associate with are bad news, and our daily lives are filled with so much stress and anxiety that our bodies just can't handle it. Noted public health physician Dr. Don Colbert, who specializes in preventative medicine, records in his book *Toxic Relief*, that otherwise healthy people are dying every day.

This slow but sure poisoning and failure to adopt healthier lifestyles is robbing us of years of life. We are laying up for ourselves lives of chronic pain, fatigue, disease and a plethora of other negative health problems that tend to manifest in people with toxic bodies. And the only one happy is the devil, the lion, whose objective is to devour! The church is no different. There are addicts in pews worldwide who knowingly choose toxic churches and refuse to adopt healthier faiths.

As in the exodus from Egypt and Babylon, the Lord is calling a remnant to separate themselves and be clean. In our environments of captivity, there are toxins that we have become accustomed to. In fact, the absence of these toxins creates feelings of discomfort and strangeness. We are comfortably contaminated and we are in need of detoxification.

Detoxification (detox) is the process of removing toxins or poison from the body. Detox is the first step for any chronic addiction. It is the process of discontinuing the drug and reducing the effects of withdrawal. The type of withdrawal effects will depend on the type of drug you have used and how long you have used it. Most people are familiar with the media's depiction of alcohol withdrawal, with some pathetic unshaven white man in his pajamas on the edge of the bed, hands trembling, trying to smoke a cigarette. Or, perhaps you have seen the media's depiction of heroin withdrawal with its aches, tremors, cold sweats, muscle cramps. Withdrawal from crack cocaine has less obvious physical manifestations, but the unseen physical damage to the physical workings of the body is devastating with long term consequences.

In addition, the psychological symptoms of withdrawal are pronounced. Dysphoria is the opposite of euphoria. Imagine the height of the feeling produced by cocaine is countered by the depth of the feeling that comes with withdrawal. Depression, anxiety, dread, paranoia, are all commonly reported psychological symptoms of withdrawal. The most difficult symptom reported by addicts is the cravings for the drug. The process of withdrawal takes from three to five days. But the cravings can last for months, even years.

Detox alone is not treatment. After a period of detoxing, the addict should undergo long-term treatment in a therapeutic community or as an outpatient, depending on the severity of his addiction. The treatment will address all aspects of addiction and will offer relapse prevention strategies. These strategies will emphasize the importance of a balanced healthy lifestyle. For you see, addiction does not only affect one's behavior, it affects one's entire lifestyle. So, detox is what the addict must do to prepare him or herself for treatment.

There are different methods of detoxing, again depending on the severity of the addiction. Some persons who are addicted to drugs will require a medical detoxification. That is, under the 24 hour/day supervision of doctors or nurses, the person is given certain drugs to assist with the symptoms of withdrawal. The drugs may be non-addicting pain medication, antidepressants, or anti-anxiety medications. These drugs are gradually discontinued. Another type of detox is to anesthetize the person so that they miss the painful physical withdrawal. Interestingly, treatment providers believe that sleeping it off is not helpful to recovery. In fact, the negative experience that comes from withdrawal is helpful to recall when an addict is contemplating returning to drug use.

Ms. M detoxed in a jail cell. She did not have the luxury of a medical facility. She endured the physiological and psychological discomforts and found safety and support in the home of her older daughter, whose plan for her mother was to love her, support her, and to share God with her through church attendance. The church did not have many persons with the same experiences as Ms. M. In fact, she would be challenged to find her place. Little did she or her daughter know that this church had many persons in it who were "church addicts" in the pews. Some pushers in the pulpit (leaders and ministers) pushed dope, and other, hope. Which would she get? I was already working in ministry with Ms. M's daughter, in the same church. Little did I know, I would meet Ms. M and that she would too become a significant part of my destiny—a focus of my calling. I was called to the least of these.

A discussion of toxicity in the church is relevant here, in order to further clarify what the recovering addict in the pew has to detox from. First, the book *Toxic Churches*, by Marc Dupont (1997), is an excellent source that exposes the beliefs, characteristics and rules of toxic faith and church addicts. Some of these were discussed earlier, such as a culture of silence, following rules without question, and a climate of mistrust. Toxic churches are abusive, significantly materialistic, manipulative and, at heart, unconcerned about the people who worship and serve. According to Dupont, persons involved in toxic environments may not be aware of the destructiveness of the system, but will likely notice that their guilt and anger increase while their self-worth decreases. This is due to the insatiable demands of the system, with little opportunities for incentives or rewards. These are the toxins that will require purification.

In an article entitled "Toxic Faith", Stanley Morris explores the intricacies of overcoming and understanding toxicity in church. As previously stated, users often don't fully comprehend the mechanics of their addictions or the need for detoxification.

"Having been misled by the seductive spirits and misdirected by control, users often are disconnected from the source of their addictions, so much so, that they rarely are able to reckon with their existence. To recover is to understand. As it pertains to religious settings, the difficulty of recovery is even greater in that the church is the VERY place sought for the recovery, while at the same time, it is the actual SOURCE of the addiction!" (Morris)

A book by the same name by Stephen Arterburn and Jack Felton (2001), describes toxic faith as,

"a destructive and dangerous relationship with a religion that allows the religion, not the relationship with God, to control a person's life." It may start out as a substitution for God but it will eventually end up being a wedge between you and the God who dearly loves you.

Are you an addict in recovery in need of detoxing? Once you have recognized your addiction through a process of the black light illumination, you decide to make a physical separation, and you are ready for detox, it should be a simple matter of 'coming to oneself' and seeking the Father. Like the prodigal son came to himself, so must every addict who seeks wholeness.

"One's personal faith should speed one's return to wholeness ...it must not be confused and distorted by legalistic, guilt-producing, institutional religion. But a climate of love, and free expression of gifts. People should not have to be burdened by a false, ill-defined, system of faith. Jesus said, "You are tired and have heavy loads. If all of you will come to me, I will give you rest. Take the job [i.e. the yoke of responsibility] that I give you. Learn from me because I am gentle and humble in heart. You will find rest for your lives. The duty I give you is easy. The load I put upon you is not heavy." (Matt. 11:28-30)" (Aterburn & Felton, 2001)

Some writers believe that you can examine the toxicity of your faith with clarity and honesty and, with intentionality, begin to remove the toxic elements through seeking God diligently and with the right accountability partners. Some choose to stay in the toxic environment as a fulfilling of their call to pray for the leaders or serve the members. If that person is not spotted and identified as a rebel, he or she may be able to withstand the pressures to stay and cooperate within the toxic system. However, if the person is identified as a rebel, or disloyal in any way, the system begins to attack, diminish, and defame character and credibility—subtly, then blatantly. For this reason, I believe that it is a risk to stay and detox. In fact, I believe that complete detoxification is only possible when complete removal has occurred. Sometimes it is necessary to remove yourself completely, in order to break free from those toxic elements.

In his book *Toxic Relief,* author Dr. Don Colbert talks about the need for restoring health and energy through fasting and detoxification. He also talks about the need to seek healthy living, away from the indoor pollution. So, when one breaks a vicious cycle like the one we've been discussing, it is not only imperative that we break the cycle physically (see previous chapter) but now that we are physically disconnected, we now need to cleanse the body. As I said earlier, once you have become toxic, you cannot transfer that kind of pollution into a clean environment.

The need for detox and restoration from a toxic faith will require that you are connected to a work of God, a move of God that specializes in deliverance, healing, and restoration. Where those areas are not addressed, there is hardly a possibility for healing and detoxification in the kingdom. So praise be to God, I am connected to healing ministries, and to persons who have strong anointings on their lives for deliverance. If you found yourself in a toxic faith, you must find yourself connected to that as well.

My detoxification process was not easy. I cried many tears, retraced many processes and procedures in my mind, second-guessed myself one hundred times, not about whether I was supposed to detach, but when and to what level. For example, was I to continue to make my consultations available to the church? Was I to tithe there until I was established? Was I to sow into the things that would bring about a healthier ministry in the former church? My heart ached for those I left behind. I wanted them to experience the same freedom that was before me. But, deep in my soul, I knew they must make their own choices with no help from me. And so, I began to detox. I began a physical program of literal dietary detoxification which included certain foods, vitamin, teas, and herbal remedies. It also included water. Lots of water!! Living water!!!

And now in my physical disconnect, and after a process of detoxification, God has relocated and planted me as senior pastor of New Dawn Restoration Center in Tampa, FL. The name is significant. New Dawn meaning former things have passed away. "BEHOLD", the Bible says, "and I shall do a new thing" (Isaiah 42:9). And so despite the pain and heartache, despite the powerlessness and hopelessness that many addicts in pews have experienced and are continuing to experience, they must recognize that beyond the present constraining four walls there is a new horizon.

God speaks of newness throughout his written Word. If any man be in Christ Jesus and of course the operative word is "in," he is a new creature. If you are celebrating personality worship you are not in Christ Jesus. When a person is found in Christ Jesus, the Bible gives you permission to become a new creation. The Bible says former things have passed away and all things are becoming new but we must be under the anointing of leaders who can walk you through the process of detoxification and healing.

When one thinks of a detox center, it is a place where addicts are taken so their systems can be cleaned out of all of the toxicity that fed their addiction and infected their bodies can be removed. It is no different in the kingdom. When one is physically disconnected from the very substance that infected you, it is not enough to quit the use of the "prophetic crack"; you must check into a spiritual detox center. New Dawn Restoration Center serves as that center and healing ground in the greater Tampa Bay-area. We find that people from churches, religions, races, creeds, ages, all over the state of Florida and all over the country are coming and finding us because they have been spiritually abused, they have been infected, infested, they have been in toxic faiths all of their lives only to realize that God really does have new mercies every morning. And they are finding that when the sun comes it is symbolic of the rising of our Lord and Savior Jesus Christ. They are finding that resurrection is possible for them. They learn that there is a resurrection that gives them a true faith, a true family, and a true future. They are finding that these things are possible for them even if there have been in the trenches of toxic faiths.

Even in the sacrament of the baptism of Christ, the going down, going under, and the coming back up is symbolic of Jesus Christ. "It is symbolic and we are beginning to live out the typology of the true meaning of Christianity and the of the sacrament of baptism and of the resurrection. That's why healing is available because He went down and came back up. And so, when we go into beautiful edifices and they throw you in water and call it baptism and you come up still demonic, then something is wrong. But, thank God, living water is available to all who will drink of it. And as Jesus told the woman at the well in John 4, "Once you take a drink of this water, you will never be thirsty again."

I have been given a couple of nicknames in the city. I laugh at them. In fact, I say if you must call me anything, at least call me "super-spiritual"; I think that's one of them. I think another one is "super-holy". Whatever the case may be, I have decided to live for Jesus and because I will not compromise the Word of the Lord for the conveniences of people. I really don't mind what I'm called or what's said of me. It does not matter. One thing I know is that the spirit of the living God rests upon New Dawn Restoration Center. He is available to everyone who walks through our doors and offered daily. Many folks in this very city will not walk through our doors because the word on the streets is, if you come in, you cannot leave the same. They fear that they will be pushed beyond their areas of comfort, and their areas of secrets, and their areas of darkness. They are afraid that their idols will be exposed like snakes in the temple and so, they just don't come in. They would be welcomed and loved like never before, if only they would come! If they came to our church, they would find a "church that is built on the solid rock," a beloved community, learning how to live a clean life.

There are other churches and movements around the country with visions similar to that of New Dawn Restoration Center. I will refer to these as safe churches. In your quest for the real thing, how must you investigate the safety of fellowship? In an article by Brenda Branson (2010), she answers the pervasive question: Are all Churches safe? And what makes them safe?

We now know that many people turn to the church for help when they are experiencing deep emotional pain from personal struggles or abusive relationships. Some have found acceptance and unconditional love from compassionate people. Others have been severely wounded by the insensitivity and judgmental attitudes in churches where guilt, manipulation, fear, and shame abound.

In his book, *Why Churches Don't Heal,* author Doug Murren writes, "Often the church is just not a safe place for us to let down our guard and be real. Imagine needing urgent medical care and getting to a hospital where you dare not admit that you have been injured! Similarly, it often seems that the last place we can admit to a personal struggle is in the church. And so we are not healed and we do not heal others."

So how can you tell the difference between a healthy church and a toxic church? According to Brenda Branson (2010), here are a few contrasts:

- A healthy church is a place where people don't hide their problems. A toxic church has a "don't ask, don't tell" atmosphere where problems are hidden and self-righteous people appear to have their lives all together.

- In a healthy church, forgiveness and grace abound. In a toxic church, people are defined and judged by the mistakes of their past.

- In a healthy church, independent thinking is encouraged and questions are welcomed. In a toxic church, people are not allowed to question the beliefs or actions of church leaders.

- Healthy church leaders invite dialogue and advice from church members. Toxic leaders prefer for people, especially women, to keep their opinions to themselves and "don't make waves".

- In a healthy church, people are taught to love God with all their heart, soul, mind and strength, and reflect

Jesus' love to others. In a toxic church, the focus is on rule-keeping, being right, and external conformity.

- In a healthy church, the pastor is transparent, admits his/her mistakes, and is accountable to a board of godly men and women. In a toxic church, the pastor has ultimate authority and is not accountable to anyone.

- In a healthy church, the pastor guides and encourages members based on biblical principles, but does not control individual decision-making. In a toxic church, the pastor tells members what to believe and how to live, demands conformity, and pressures members to break fellowship with others who don't share their beliefs or meet their standards.

- In a healthy church, men and women are given equal respect and biblical roles of responsibility at church and in the home. Abuse of any kind is not tolerated. In a toxic church, women are considered subservient and are expected to submit to everything their husbands demand. Many women in abusive marriages are told stay with their abuser, cook his favorite meals, be more submissive, and pray harder.

I've alluded to this earlier and it bears repeating here. There are many churches that are functioning well and are without toxicity. No church does everything correctly. Good practices and great leaders are found even in the most toxic churches. So one must be careful about how one evaluates any ministry. There are many examples of healthy mega churches to follow. Some that have caught my attention over the years are: Saddleback in various locations in CA; Ray of Hope in Atlanta; New Creation Christian Fellowship in San Antonio, TX; and Beth Rapha in Pomona, NY. Likewise, there are wonderful small churches doing great things for the Lord. It is my prayer that readers will not use this book as a tool for indictment, but as a means for further discernment, and correction.

As you find healing and safety in a church community, reach out to others who may be struggling so they may experience love and acceptance as God's life flows through you.

Personal Reflections:

I work out at least four times per week. As a result, my system is acclimated to a regimented diet and to frequent and deliberate acts of detoxification. I have noticed that as my body rids itself of toxins, I am always amazed at how much is yet "in" me. When I first began I was appalled! How could my body hold all these toxins and still remain functional? It made me realize the absolute necessity of continuous detoxification and the absolute necessity of remaining clean.

I have been in church all my life. I have been faithful to the service of the Lord all my life. How could my spirit man be in such bad shape...full of toxins? We are corrupted and influenced heavily by that which we allow to enter our systems. Just as I chose to exercise and eat right, not as a resolution but as a lifestyle, I have chosen to do the same in my spiritual life. It is necessary for me to detox of all that I know to be corrupt in my system. It is necessary for me to detox of all that has proven to render me unhealthy. It is necessary for me to rid my life of all the toxic influence, toxic people, and toxic doctrine that I know serves to corrupt my spirit man.

Jesus, desire for us is to live holy and He says that it is possible, for He is holy. I choose to put more and more of Him in my spirit as opposed to the negativity of this world. I choose to be saturated in Him, by Him and for Him. I choose to detox!

1. What are you willing to do to begin the process of physical and spiritual detoxification?

2. Are you willing to fast, and pray to allow God to reveal to you if you are in a safe church?

3. If you are a leader or pastor, will you allow God to speak to you regarding the safety of your church?

CHAPTER TWELVE

LIVING A CLEAN LIFE:
AND SERIOUS ABOUT IT

"And they came to Jericho: and as he went out of Jericho with his disciples and a great number of people, blind Bartimaeus, the son of Timaeus, sat by the highway side begging. And when he heard that it was Jesus of Nazareth, he began to cry out, and say, Jesus, thou son of David, have mercy on me. And many charged him that he should hold his peace: but he cried the more a great deal, Thou son of David, have mercy on me. And Jesus stood still, and commanded him to be called. And they call the blind man, saying unto him, Be of good comfort, rise; he calleth thee. And he, casting away his garment, rose, and came to Jesus. And Jesus answered and said unto him, What wilt thou that I should do unto thee? The blind man said unto him, Lord, that I might receive my sight. And Jesus said unto him, Go thy way; thy faith hath made thee whole. And immediately he received his sight, and followed Jesus in the way." (Mark 10:46-52)

Mark shares the story of a man who was physically blind, who had the tenacity and audacity to pursue Jesus Christ. He tells this story to draw the stark comparison to the blind man's faith, and spiritual sight compared to the leader's lack of faith and spiritual blindness.

To have sight is a wonderful blessing. Of course it enables us to see the world around us, clothed in its majesty with all its complexities and beauty. Sight affords us the ability to experience visually God's splendor on the earth. Sight allows us to embrace nature and the universe and all of its infinite mystery.

"But there is a different kind of sight. We know about it because of the teachings in the scriptures. This sight that comes more from the center of our being, and drives home the truth of all things, is a gift of the Spirit. It allows us to feel the reality of a thing for ourselves. It permits us to look past the temporal sense of 'sight' and weigh it within our heart. It blesses us with the ability and sensibility to accept the principles that are far higher and loftier than the things easily "seen" in the world around us. This is the sight we should aspire to have. With this ability, the eyes are not so easily fooled and the heart can direct us in the paths of righteousness the Savior wants us to travel. We can use the eyes as the "jewel of the body" to savor the good things in this life, while looking forward to even better things hereafter!" (Henry David Thoreau cited by Taylor)

"Amazing grace, how sweet the sound, that saved a wretch like me! I once was lost, but now I'm found; was blind, but now I see."

"It is the Lord's good grace that takes us, mortal and blinded and lost, and molds us with the gentle love and goodness that is built upon eternal principles and Godly love. His ways are sure. His sight is perfect.

Although the world may close in around us and our sight be dim, His light keeps right on leading the way. Fears are replaced with a comfort that only comes with His truth. With that truth, our vision increases." (Taylor, *I Once Was Blind, But Now I See*)

Recovery is a process. The first step in the process is opening spiritual eyes to the moral, ethical, and righteous blind spots that have supported the addiction. Much has been written about a 12-step recovery process.

The secret of recovery, of overcoming addiction, will involve two very distinct areas of conviction. One, to accept the revelation and illumination that brings sight to see that which has been disguised; and two, to make a consistent set of decisions to abstain from that which had controlled our lives. We can dress this up in any number of ways. But the core of recovery, be it spiritual or otherwise, must be acting based upon what we now see (revelation knowledge) and abstinence, and that requires consistent decision-making. Consciously choosing recovery and sobriety, and deciding to stay clean and sober and sticking with it, is no simple task. Each day of sobriety brings new opportunity. This is a double-edged sword, because the possibility of relapse is constantly lurking for those who are clean. We have to decide each and every day to abstain from chemicals. Anyone who is struggling to get through their first 30 days clean can attest to this fact. And so we work 12-step programs and practice spiritual principles in order to deal with our life in the face of abstinence. But in the beginning, it is a struggle, because we can clearly see that it was not just a single decision that was needed in order to achieve sobriety, but a daily decision that we would have to face every day. (Patrick, 2008, *Making a Decision For Recovery*)

The path to relapse is filled with apparently irrelevant decisions, says a psychologist friend of mine. People don't wake up one day and decide, I will smoke crack again. They make subtle choices; seemingly unrelated behaviors that lead to errors. For example, they decide to visit a friend that they heard was sick in the old neighborhood. While there, someone passes them a joint. Rather than leave the scene, they stay, using willpower to resist; but inhaling the familiar aroma brings back an all too familiar craving. Decisions must be made carefully each day.

It is very common to hear a person who is recovering state that they live one day at a time. Sometimes it feels like an hour at a time, or even five minutes at a time. As time progresses, the life of a recovering addict gets easier. Most point to spirituality and credit their relationship with an all-knowing, all-loving, all-powerful, and all-forgiving Savior as being the one thing that kept them clean. Many have tried family, friends, and even treatment programs, but until they realized that their will and problems had to be released completely to God for handling, they were stuck in their addictions.

When Ms. M was asked about some of the things that kept her clean, she immediately listed her family members, grandchildren, children, and her mother, who was in the final stages of life and deteriorating.

"I couldn't stand the chance that I would be locked up in prison and my mother pass away, and it was nothing I could do about it. It was one promise I made when I was in jail the last time, if I get out of this, I want my mother to see me clean, before she dies. And she did. Five years; I had been clean five years before she died."

When asked where her strength comes from, Ms. M said, "My strength comes from God. I stay in my Bible. I'm in church. And that's it, by the grace of God, by the grace of God that I am sitting here now. I say I could have been dead. I should have been dead. I stay in my Bible."

Let's parallel this challenge to live clean with the life of the addict in the pew. Choosing to detach and detox from that which has proven itself to be unhealthy is no easy task. But the moment one makes the decision, just on the other side of the exit, God has an entrance with a plethora of opportunities! It is particularly difficult if it involves a church where one has sown their very lives and livelihood; where the investment stakes were high; and the levels of loyalty and faithfulness were never questioned. This can be, and was for me, a very difficult transition.

In the best of circumstances, the enemy launches attacks against God's people. These attacks may be replete with character assassinations, false allegations, and unmerited fault-finding, all because the spirit of control has been aroused and angered. The spirit of control causes the affected leader to demand a false sense of loyalty from all who serve him or her. It demands agreement with all "important" dogma originating from the leader, even those that may be biblically or morally wrong. So, the warning is this: hear the Word of the Lord and heed to it. But be aware that in the face of sound decisions, there will yet be attacks. Even when motives are pure, the enemy will take root in demented spirits seeking to cause continued confusion, dissension and division. And, after all, isn't that his job? Revelation knowledge can be very dangerous. Our encouragement is to operate carefully, understanding it's not about putting other fellowships down or cursing their existence, but it's about satisfying a hunger and thirst after righteousness that God Himself has birthed in your appetite.

I asked Ms. M, who has so graciously allowed her powerful testimony to be reflected throughout the book, "Is it difficult living a clean life?" She summed it up well. She simply said "No, it is not difficult to live a clean life. I have decided not to be influenced by negative people any longer." Other addicts echo a very common piece of wisdom learned in treatment centers around the world; do not return to old people, places, and things! So when one makes a decision to live clean, my advice to you is to surround yourself with God-fearing, God-believing people who study their Bibles, and who understand that they are not to sit in the seat of the scoffer, nor to stand in the presence of sinners. And, understand you must break that camp and disconnect from receiving counsel from the ungodly (Psalm 1).

Psalm 1 clearly gives us the parallel and states that when you disconnect, you will be like a tree planted by the waters and everything you touch shall prosper. That's what I am experiencing in my life right now. I conclude from all of my research, from Psalm 1, and my own experience that in order to live a clean life, if you are going to stay clean, don't allow others to contaminate you. The Word of the Lord says that bad company corrupts good morals (1 Corinthians 15:33). Therefore I make a conscious decision, and I don't eat lunch with them. I don't go to parties with them. I don't open Christmas gifts with them. I simply pray for them and live my life clean, from a distance.

For that matter, they can call me what they want to; my God calls me faithful. And for that I am grateful, honored, and glad. To live a clean life, make a decision to protect your personal space. My life has changed dramatically because I understand now that I not only know Him (as Paul stated in the Bible) in the fellowship of His suffering, but I also know Him in the power of the resurrection and that should be the quest for everybody who says they love God. I once was blind, but now I see. Morning by morning, I witness a fresh new dawn in my life. There is a new dawn for you as well. Amen.

Reflection:

1. Are you a victim of "prophetic crack"?

2. Are you ready for the new dawn in your life?

3. What are some people, places, and things you already know you must let go of?

BIBLIOGRAPHY

Achtemeier, P. J. & Society of Biblical Literature Ed.). (1985). *Harper's Bible Dictionary* (Revised). New York: Harper and Rowe.

Arterburn, S. & Felton J. (2001). *Toxic Faith*. Colorado Springs, CO: Waterbrook Press.

Beattie, M. (1987). *Codependent No More: How to Stop Controlling Others and Start Caring for Yourself* (1992 edition). Center City, MN: Hazelden Publishers.

Berne, E. (1964). *Games People Play*. New York: Ballantine Books.

Bill, N. (2004, June 12). Finding The Perfect Church Was Never The Issue. Retrieved from http://www.hirotao.blogspot.com/

Boa, K. (Retrieved June 2008). Dependence on God. Retrieved from http://www.Bible.org/seriespage/dependence-god.

Brace, R. (Retrieved June 2008). How Can I Discern Whether I'm in a Healthy or Abusive Fellowship? Retrieved from http://homepage.ntlworld.com/robin.brace/abusive-group.htm

Branson, B. (2010). Are All Churches Safe? Retrieved from http://www.peaceandsafety.com

Burney, R. (1995) *Codependence: The Dance of Wounded Souls*. (First edition). Cambria, CA: Joy To You & Me Enterprises

Burney, R. (1998) *Wounded Souls Dancing in The Light.* (First edition). Cambria, CA: Joy To You & Me Enterprises

Cash, M. (Retrieved June, 2008). Codependency in the Church: The Dysfunctional Family of God. Retrieved from http://margiecash.com/publications/codependency-in-the-church-the-dysfunctional-family-of-god

Cauley, K. (Retrieved June, 2008). Modern Day Idolatry. Retrieved from http://preachersfiles.com/modern-day-idolatry/ Church and Capitalism. (May 13, 2008). Retrieved from http://shadowsofthedivine.blogspot.com/2008_05_01_archive.html

Dupont, M. A. (1997). *Toxic Churches: Restoration From Spiritual Abuse.* (2004 edition). Grand Rapids, MI: Chosen Books, A Division of Baker Book House Co.

Enroth, R. (1994). *Recovering From Churches That Abuse.* Grand Rapids, MI: Zondervan Publishing House

Friel, J. C. & Friel, L. D. (1988). *Adult Children: The Secrets of Dysfunctional Families.* Deerfield Beach, FL: Health Communications, Inc.

Friel, J. & Subby, R. (1984). Co-Dependency in the Church: The Dysfunctional Family of God. Retrieved from http://margiecash.com/publications/codependency-in-the-church-the-Dysfunctional-family-of-god/

Henzel, R. They Told Me That If I Left. Retrieved from http://www.batteredsheep.com/they_told.html

Hoke, D. (1994). Thinking Biblically About Idolatry - Exodus 20: 4-6. Retrieved from http://www.mountainretreatorg.net/articles/idol.html

Howey, P. The Danger of the Traditions of Men. Retrieved from http://www.truthguard.com/Articles/the-danger-of-the-traditions-of-men-a6.html

Imbach, J. (1998). *The River Within: Loving God, Living Passionately,* Fresh Wind Press

Jenkins-Hall, K (2004). Simplify: A woman's diet for spiritual and emotional fitness. Tampa, FL: NdueCzon Publishing Group.

Joyner, R. (Retrieved June, 2008). Overcoming Witchcraft. Retrieved from http://www.upstreamca.org/ocwitchcraft.html

Knapp, P. Aberrant Christianity: What Is It? Retrieved from http://www.gospeloutreach.net/aberrant.html

Lewis, A. (2005) Overcoming Addiction—Addiction + Denial = Out of Control. Retrieved from http://ezinearticles.com/?expert=Angie+Lewis&opt=ecats&ecat=Self-Improvement:Addictions

The Lockman Foundation (1977a). The Gospel according to John. New American Standard Bible (The Open Bible ed., pp. 1010-1039). New York, NY: Thomas Nelson.

The Lockman Foundation (1977b). The Epistle of Paul to the Ephesians. New American Standard Bible (The Open Bible ed., pp. 1129-1135). New York, NY: Thomas Nelson.

The Lockman Foundation (1977c). The Epistle to the Hebrews. New American Standard Bible (The Open Bible ed., pp. 1169-1183). New York, NY: Thomas Nelson.

May, G. (1988). *Addiction and Grace* (Reissue). San Francisco: Harper San Francisco.

Morris, S. Toxic Faith. Retrieved from http://www.theexaminer.org/volume8/number5/toxic.html

Narcanon International. (2010). What is Crack? Retrieved from http://www.narconon.ca/crack.htm

Narconon International. Crack Cocaine Information. What Are Crack's Adverse Effects? Retrieved from http://www.narconon.org/drug/information/cocaine-crack.html

Orton, D. (2004). *Snakes In The Temple: Unmasking Idolatry In Today's Church And Pointing The Way to Spiritual Breakthrough*. Lancaster, U.K.: Sovereign World Publishers Ltd.

Patrick. (2008). Making a Decision From Recovery. Retrieved from http://www.spiritualriver.com

Porcello, J. Legalism Recovery. Retrieved from http://ourfellowship.org/recovery.html

Rudd, S. Drugs and the Bible: E; Shrooms, Cocaine, Crack, Maraijuana. Retrieved from http://www.bible.ca/s-marijuana.htm

Rutland, M. (1987). *Launch Out into the Deep*. Franklin Springs, GA: Advocate Press.

Schaef, A. W. (1990). "Is the Church an Addictive Organization"? *Christian Century Magazine*, pp. 18-21.

Schaef, A. W. (1986). *Co-Dependence Misunderstood—Mistreated*. San Francisco, CA: Harper-Collins Publishers.

Scott, B. Church Edifices: Are They Our Idols? Retrieved from http://www.mindspring.com/~renewal/Idolatry.html

Should Pastors Rule Over You? (December 5, 2006). Retrieved from King James Translator's Notes. Retrieved from http://bible.cc/colossians/2-8.htm

Subby, R. (1984). Inside the Chemically Dependent Marriage: Denial and Manipulation. Retrieved from http://books.google.com

Taylor, V. I Once Was Blind But Now I See. *Meridian Magazine*. Retrieved from http://www.ldsmag.net/candoyouth/index.html

Wedge, M. (n.d.). Religious legalism and its adverse affects on Christians. Retrieved from http://www.factnet.org/cults/Toxic_Faith/Religious_Legalism.html

Wesley, J. (August 7, 2010). John Wesley's Notes on the Bible. Retrieved from http://wesley.nnu.edu/john_wesley/notes/

Wesley, J. (2007). Overcoming Addiction and Escapism. Retrieved from http://www.pickthebrain.com/blog/overcoming-addiction-by-escaping-escapism

West Penn Allegheny Health System. (2009). Addiction and Co-dependency. Health Topics A-Z. Retrieved from http://www.wpahs.org/patients/health/index.cfm?mode=view&healthtopic=197

Whitfield, C. L. (1984). *Codependency: An emerging problem.* Co-Dependency (pp. 47-57). Deerfield Beach, FL: Health Communications.